P9-CAY-999

DISCARD

Barrett Willoughby
Alaska's Forgotten Lady

Jefferson County Library
dar Avenue
'^ 98339
v.info

TE DUE

Posed portrait of Barrett Willoughby. *Courtesy of Ruth Taylor*

Barrett Willoughby
Alaska's Forgotten Lady

Nancy Warren Ferrell

UNIVERSITY OF ALASKA PRESS

Library of Congress Cataloging-in-Publication Data

Ferrell, Nancy Warren.
    Barrett Willoughby : Alaska's forgotten lady / Nancy Warren
Ferrell.
        p.   cm.
    Includes bibliographical references.
    ISBN 0-912006-76-5 : $14.95
    1. Willoughby, Barrett, d. 1959.   2. Women and literature--Alaska-
-History--20th century.   3. Women authors, American--20th century-
-Biography.   4. Women authors, American--Alaska--Biography.
    5. Women pioneers--Alaska--Biography.   6. Alaska--Intellectual life.
    7. Alaska--In literature.   I. Title.
    PS3545.I5785Z65   1994
    813'.52--dc20
    [B]   94-34537
                                                                        CIP

© 1994 by Nancy Warren Ferrell
All rights reserved. First Printing
International Standard Book Number: paper, ISBN 0-912006-76-5
Library of Congress Catalogue Number: 94-34537

Printed in the United States of América by Thomson-Shore, Inc.

This publication was printed on acid-free paper that meets the minimum requirements for
the American National Standard for Information Science—Permanence of Paper for Printed
Library Materials ANSI Z39.48-1984

Publication coordination by Pamela Odom.
Cover and book design by Paula Elmes, Publications Center, Center for Cross-Cultural
Studies.
Production by Jennifer Thompson.

This book is dedicated to early women pioneers and particularly recognizes the part they played in developing Alaska and Canada.

Contents

Acknowledgments

I am grateful to so many people for help on this project over the past ten years. In that time, some of my personal sources have passed away.

I liken the gathering of book material to a series of contacts—one person passing me on to another.

Inez Gregg of Juneau told me of Helen Smith Scudder in California, who was the source for much of the personal material concerning Willoughby. From the start, Helen picked over her memory, and her belongings, for anything which might help.

From the onset, historian Robert DeArmond, now of Sitka, gave what help he could, from memory and from his files.

Colleague Carol Beery Davis of Juneau, shared her experiences. Carol led me to Patricia Charles of Ketchikan.

Frank Homan of Juneau led me to Carol Sturgulewski of Unalaska, who led me to Elsa Pedersen of Sterling. All stretched their memories for me, and filled in missing Willoughby data.

Betty Pfouts of the Jefferson County Historical Society in Port Townsend, Washington, not only helped with material, but Betty led me to Joan Buhler who led me to Jim Hermanson. They all kept my project in mind and assisted in some way.

Talking with Gen Harmon of Juneau led me to Merion Cass Frolich on the East Coast. Merion shared her mother's photos.

Publisher Bob Henning of Washington State searched his memory and came up with some useful Willoughby material.

Miriam Hilscher of Anchorage led me to Robert Atwood. Carolyn Burg of Juneau led me to Ruth Taylor.

Some detective work led me to Willoughby's niece and namesake in Washington, D.C., who again, gave me insights about her aunt. Author Lucile McDonald of Washington State further helped when contacted. So, too, did Sister M. Ann Sullivan of Seattle. Ted Merrell, Jr., of Juneau helped with photos.

Many libraries, newspapers, historical societies, and state/private agencies on the West Coast and Canada contributed to this book. Specifically, I thank Director Kay Shelton and her staff of the Alaska State Historical Library in Juneau. Thanks also to the staff of the Rasmuson Library, University of Alaska Fairbanks, especially Renee Blahuta. At the Juneau Public Library where I work, Susan Van Dusseldorp was particularly helpful in securing information.

It seems the people closest to the author are usually mentioned last. Certainly this is courtesy to others, not casualness. My husband, Ed Ferrell, helped with research and editing, and did it with enthusiasm. My victories were his victories; my disappointments, his, too. Thanks, Ed.

—Nancy W. Ferrell

1

A True Alaskan

Jack London and Rex Beach established the image of Alaska as a land of snow and cold. Theirs were the exciting stories of adventure and of life and death struggles to gain riches. Jet travel and television to the contrary, that image of Alaska subtly remains.

There was a woman writer, too—a contemporary of London and Beach—who wrote of Alaskan life one step beyond the stampeder.

> [S]he clearly pictures in no uncertain words the call of the North to the children of the North—the taking up of life by the second generation when their fathers have pioneered the way. . . . [1]

Her name was Barrett Willoughby. She portrayed the territory in its broadest sense—its variety of weather and land, its many industries and cultures, its inhabitants. In a way, she captured a truer image of Alaska than did London or Beach, although she never sold as many books, nor received as much acclaim. Willoughby did, however, enjoy a national and international standing during her career.

That a woman would write about Alaska was more unusual when considered in the context of the times; women had been given the vote only two years before Willoughby's first novel came out in 1922. Alaska was isolated; the territory might have been a little-known foreign country for its remoteness. Alaska was a man's world; the image of weather, adventures and wealth had been set during the gold stampedes and remained in the minds of non-Alaskans.

Regardless of Wisconsin birth, Barrett Willoughby can be considered an Alaskan, living more than twenty years of her early life in the Cook Inlet area of southcentral Alaska. Later she resided in California, returning to Alaska to gather material for her books and articles. Every piece she published in her career had an Alaskan setting. Barrett Willoughby was one of the first published Alaskan fiction authors to receive international recognition. And she was the first Alaskan woman to do so.

"It is claimed," wrote the *Cordova Daily Times*, "that Barrett Willoughby is the first real Alaskan novelist. . . . "[2]

Yet today she is all but forgotten.

There was a time when Willoughby earned a global reputation through her writings and contributed a flavor of romance and adventure to Alaska's image. During the first half of the twentieth century, Willoughby penned numerous articles for national magazines, seven romantic novels, three nonfiction books, and two travelogues—all with an Alaskan backdrop. Several of her books were printed by British publishers, were used in classrooms in the United States, were printed in Braille for the blind, and were translated into foreign languages.[3] Hollywood made two of her novels—*Rocking Moon* and *Spawn of the North*—into movies.

For her subject matter, for her time in history, Willoughby was a major writer. Like her contemporaries

Studio portrait of Barrett Willoughby taken in San Francisco before 1930. Here Willoughby calls herself the "Eskimo Pie." *Courtesy of Helen Smith Scudder*

Publicity photograph published in the *Los Angeles Examiner*, November 17, 1931. *Hearst Collection, Department of Special Collections, University of Southern California Library*

London and Beach, Willoughby was no armchair author; she lived many of the experiences she later described. And, in contrast to the other two authors, Willoughby's many years in Alaska gave her a broad base for authentic Alaskan writings.

2

A Father's Legacy

Perhaps the person most influencing Willoughby's life and later work was her father, Martin Barrett, whom she described as " . . . one of those Irishmen, debonair, fearless, and gay, who are born to adventure as the sea gull to the sea."[1]

The male characters in Barrett Willoughby's novels, too, were patterned after her father. They were usually dashing, powerful, keen, genial—a law unto themselves. Just as her father was called "Wild Martin," she nicknamed many of her fiction fathers— Daredevil Dick Clonard the flyer;[2] the Fighting Priest;[3] and a grandfather figure, Dynamite Danny O'Moore the seining captain.[4]

Little was documented of Martin Barrett's early years. He was born in Waterford, Ireland, in March 1846,[5] arriving in the United States, according to Barrett Willoughby, at the age of eight. Spending two years with a grandmother in New Orleans and one year with an uncle in Chicago, Martin then was hired at the age of eleven as a cabin boy aboard steamships plying the Mississippi River. At thirteen he traveled west to California. For the next twenty years a gambler's hope took him from one mining discovery to another through the west.[6]

While Martin roamed the country, his future wife, Florence Clink (Klink), was born in Germany in March of 1867.[7] Eventually she traveled to America, and more particularly to Wisconsin. By the age of thirty-seven, perhaps Martin was more willing to settle down, for love drew him to the petite seventeen-year-old Florence. In 1883 the two were wed in Berlin, Wisconsin.[8]

If Florence had any idea of settling down with her husband, it soon vanished. The same year they married, the Barretts moved to Spokane to open a hotel, but this venture did not succeed. Two years later Martin and Florence returned to Berlin, Wisconsin, where Martin found employment with his brother-in-law. This work relationship lasted three years.[9]

No sooner had the Barretts returned to Wisconsin than their first child, Lawrence, was born—about 1884–1885.[10] Their second child and namesake to her mother, Florence—the future Barrett Willoughby—was born in May of 1886.[11]

Young Florence's birthplace and birth date have never been verified through official vital statistics. And, it seems, Barrett Willoughby fostered this obscure past.[12] Biographical information about Barrett Willoughby on book flaps and in interviews said she was "Alaskan by birth, and early upbringing. . . . "[13]

In later life, Barrett Willoughby managed to take at least ten years off her age. No one could prove otherwise, and it seemed a harmless vanity.

Helen Smith Scudder, who had been a young girl during their shared days in Katalla said she (Helen) was born in 1899, and at the time, young Florence Barrett was at least ten years older.[14] The 1910 U.S. Census stated that young Florence had a May 1886 birthday, and Helen's information supported that figure.

Two years after Florence's birth in Wisconsin, Martin moved his family to Washington State. There the last Barrett, Frederick, was born in May of 1892.[15]

Little was known of the family's next four years. Rumors of Klondike gold drew the family north. Obviously Martin's hunger for adventure had not died, for when an opportunity to procure a schooner—the *Leslie*—developed, Martin, Steve Roe, Captain Lyons, and Thomas Lane outfitted the ship and sailed north from Washington shores. The rest of the Barrett family was also on board.[16] With little more than hope and an able ship, the crew prospected the Alaskan coast as far as Cook Inlet. It might be assumed that the Barrett family spent some time in the Sitka area, as Florence later wrote of details there, experienced when she was young.[17]

Memories from this voyage remained with young Florence for the rest of her life. She used portions in later books, and her adventures proved far from the ordinary: she told of hostile Indians and totems, of screaming winds and towering waves, of becalmed waters and glaciated mountains.[18] Regardless of dangerous weather, animals, or people, young Florence had complete faith in her father: "Nothing could happen to us while Dad stood out there at the unhoused wheel. . . ."[19]

One of Martin's adventures, however, nearly proved fatal for the Barretts. In 1896 the family, with Captain Lyons, was marooned for ten months on barren Middleton Island. The spot was a storm-racked island in the Gulf of Alaska, seventy-five miles from the mainland.[20] There were few if any trees on the island and no land animals. Even birds and sea animals found more congenial spots to spend the winter. Ships avoided the island because of dangerous shores, so the Barretts held little hope of signaling for rescue.

Landing there in September to prospect for gold, Martin sold the schooner on the promise that the ship would return and take them off in a short time. For some reason, the vessel failed to return, and the Barretts and Lyons barely survived the winter and starvation. They

Aerial view of Middleton Island, Alaska. *Courtesy of T. R. Merrell, Jr., National Marine Fisheries*

View of Federal Aviation Administration station and runway on Middleton Island. *Courtesy of T. R. Merrell, Jr., National Marine Fisheries*

Abandoned dory on the beach of Middleton Island, Alaska.
Courtesy of T. R. Merrell, Jr., National Marine Fisheries

Middleton Island, west boundary, with driftwood on the beach.
Courtesy of T. R. Merrell, Jr., National Marine Fisheries

lived on waterlogged flour, limpets, and what rations they had brought along, until a cannery tender rescued them the following June.[21]

In 1907, Martin told a gathering of Katalla pioneers about the experience.[22] At that time, someone asked: "How about eating those boots?"

"They make good soup," returned Martin Barrett.

The Middleton experience, seen through the ten-year-old eyes of young Florence Barrett, was an adventure rather than a near fatal tragedy. As an adult, she chronicled the experience in *Gentlemen Unafraid*. In the book she said it was the children's habit while on Middleton to make up and dramatize stories:

> [O]ur chief joy was the serial story composed verbally by my oldest brother Loll (Lawrence). . . . I remember my baby brother was Admiral Captain Freddie of the Rocking Horse Brigade. I was the rather wooden heroine deprived of any voluntary action because I was being rescued all the time.[23]

Perhaps the Middleton winter, with imagination the only toy, helped to nurture a creativity in Florence which she later used in writings as Barrett Willoughby.

Once rescued from Middleton and on the mainland again, the family did not have time to consider their ordeal. It was 1897, and this time Martin was in the right place at the right time to satisfy his adventuring spirit. The Klondike Gold Rush was on, and the Barretts lost no time traveling to Dawson, in Canada's Yukon Territory. Only a few months after his rescue from Middleton—September 14, 1897—Martin "of Dawson," laid claim to No. 16 on Victoria Gulch in the Yukon District, Canada.[24]

How long Martin worked the claim was not known, for the family was not heard from again until *Polk's Alaska-*

Dawson City, Yukon Territory, Canada in 1900 when the Barretts made it their home. Young Florence and her brother, Lawrence, boarded in Seattle schools during the winters. *Historical Photograph Collection, Rasmuson Library, University of Alaska Fairbanks*

Yukon Directory recorded the adults Martin and Florence as living in Dawson, in 1901. Martin was listed as a miner.[25]

By that time, the Barretts had begun what can be termed "the Alaska commute"; they spent the winter months "Outside" in warmer locales while remaining in the north during the summer months. Thus, though records show Martin and wife Florence as residing in Dawson during 1901 and 1902,[26] a Dawson post office clerk recorded Martin sailing south September 25, 1901,[27] only to be listed back in Dawson in 1902.[28]

Lawrence and young Florence boarded in Catholic schools in King County, near Seattle, during that period. Lawrence, about fifteen or sixteen at the time, was educated at the College of Our Lady of Lourdes,[29] while Florence, then fourteen, studied several years at the

For part of her education, Florence Barrett boarded at the Academy of the Holy Names on Seventh and Jackson Streets, Seattle, during her mid-teen years. The Academy was razed in 1908 to make way for a growing business district. *Courtesy of Holy Names Academy, Seattle, Washington*

Academy of the Holy Names.[30] Florence herself mentioned that she spent some earlier years attending Catholic convent schools in San Francisco, which could be fact. However, the California Archdiocese had no school records of that period.[31]

Such were the early years of young Florence Barrett. She lived a carefree, ever-changing existence in unusual and exciting places. At the same time, she thrived on such an existence. Florence developed a romantic view of life; she tended to look at ordeals as adventures and found positive attributes in challenging experiences. Financial security was a matter of "luck," and took second place to impulse. In 1900, when females were expected to be dependent on others and to know their place, Florence was developing a more independent outlook.

She acquired a strong love for Alaska, later allowing readers to think it her birthplace. Her enthusiasm for the north was expressed in one of her books:

> Life is a wonderful gift in sunny Alaska, and
> I have little sympathy with . . . tales that have
> made the very name of our country a synonym
> for cold and ugliness. To me Alaska stands for
> youth, romance, and beauty.[32]

Barrett Willoughby in Katalla, Alaska, at 17 years old. The photograph is dated 1904. *Franklin R. Brenneman Collection, Alaska State Library, Juneau*

3

A Settled Home in Katalla

As if the excitement of gold were not enough, rich deposits of copper were discovered in the Wrangell Mountains of southcentral Alaska. Soon after, coal and oil were found. From that time on, two towns-to-be—Cordova and Katalla (sometimes spelled Catalla)—competed to attract railroad investment and construction to the interior.[1]

Dawson gold mining must not have been going well, because Martin Barrett and his family headed south to the coast. He, along with several hundred newcomers, cast his hope of financial return with Katalla, which was established in 1903.[2] Perhaps his age, too—then in his mid-fifties—called for a more rooted home life. With what money he possessed, he became owner of a general merchandise store, a hotel, and a restaurant in Katalla and settled down with his family.[3]

Katalla, fifty miles from its Cordova rival, developed into a small coastal community. There was fierce competition between the two towns, each vying to be shipping port for the interior copper mines. When *The Katalla Herald* newspaper came into existence, its banner headline shouted: "KATALLA, THE COMING METROPOLIS OF ALASKA, WHERE THE RAILS MEET THE SAILS."

Outside the F. M. Barrett General Store, Katalla, Alaska. *Barrett Willoughby Photograph Collection, Rasmuson Library, University of Alaska Fairbanks*

The main disadvantage of the town proved to be weather; raging storms racked the community, preventing ships from landing or loading.

Even in those early years, young Florence seemed interested in words. First public mention of her was in the December 21, 1903, issue of the *Catalla Drill* when she was seventeen years old:

> We understand Miss Florence M. Barrette, professional stenographer and typewriter, is preparing to do work in her line for those requiring her services. She can be found at her father's restaurant on D Street.[4]

Florence subsequently obtained a job as one of the clerks in the Commissioner's Court for Kayak Precinct, of which

KATALLA HERALD

HE COMING METROPOLIS OF ALASKA, WHERE THE RAILS MEET THE SAILS

KATALLA, ALASKA, SATURDAY, AUGUST 22, 1908   PRICE TEN CENTS

nery all ready for operation next spring; and it is also reported that a whaling station is to be located here in the near future, which will make Yakutat a busy little place next spring."

Alaska's New Game Law

Alaska has a new game law, passed at the last session of congress, and as it is now a law of the land, its provisions, so far as they are related to this section of the territory, will be of interest to hunters and others. The open season, that is the season during which it is lawful to kill game, is as follows: Moose, caribou and mountain sheep, from August 20 to December 31, both inclusive; brown bear from October 1 to July 1, both inclusive; deer and mountain goats from April 1 to February 1, both inclusive; grouse, ptarmigan, shore birds and water fowl from September 1 to March 1, both inclusive.

THE PROMISE OF STILLWATER

Charles Doughten who went outside recently is doing his part in making the Katalla coal fields known and respected abroad. In an interview in a Seattle paper he is quoted thus: "The quality of coal taken from that district is as good as any coal mined in the United States. I believe that when the railroad is built from Stillwater to Kanak island, Stillwater will be the Pittsburg of Alaska. I have spent all my life in the coal fields, beginning when I was a boy in the Pocahontas district o' Virginia. At that time people thought that coal would not pay in Virginia, but now it is producing the best coal in the country. Alaska coal is of exceptionally fine quality. All that is lacking is transportation. Stillwater is thirty miles from Katalla, which is a few miles from Kanak island. A bridge could be built across Bering river and a railroad built from Kanak island to Stillwater, which will open a rich district. I believe that the Guggenheims see this, for it is rumored that they are contemplating tapping that country. The rumor states that they will build from Kanak island north. I understand that T. P. McDonald, of the Bering lake district, has a contract with the government to furnish 200,000 tons of coal. I will go back into that country soon."

MR. ECCLES AN ALASKA BOOSTER

on earth. The deposits cover an area of 125 square miles, and he saw seams of coal from eight to 69 feet in extent, and plenty of them. The deposits are about thirty miles from tidewater, presenting an ideal proposition for development on an enormous scale."

Shepard Creek is Promising

Judge Britton and O. L. Willoughby returned Sunday night from a trip to Shepard creek, in the coal belt. Judge Britton says that some splendid coal has been taken out of the English company's mine on Carbon creek. There are also fine coal outcroppings on the west branch of Shepard creek, and the indications are that Shepard creek will develop into a fine coal area. Transportation facilities can be easily provided as the grades are easy and a railroad would have no engineering difficulties to overcome.

REGISTERED MAIL IS MISSING

In the last two months four packages of registered mail, from Seattle for Katalla, have disappeared somewhere along the route, that is if they left Seattle. One of these packages containing forty-two pieces of registered mail was not received at the local office on the Portland arriving here July 17. Postmaster Williams checked up the mail and then reported its non arrival here to the department. On the last trip of the Portland two more registered packages failed to reach the postoffice, but Mr. Williams has no record of the number of pieces. The purser of the Portland says he receipted for the mail in Seattle, but the fact remains that it never reached the Katalla postoffice. In its worse than niggardly treatment of this place the department makes no provision for carrying the mail between the mail steamers and the postoffice, and it has been brought ashore through the courtesy of the tug boat captains. If there is a more utterly rotten mail service on the face of the earth than that supplied Katalla by this billion-dollar-a-year government The Herald would like to hear of it.

Ladies and Gents' Furnishing Goods—C. J. Dykes, Post Office B'ldg.

COAL AND OIL FAIR EXHIBITS

NEWS OF KOYUKUK

Few Men Have Gone Into The Country

The Herald is in receipt of a letter from George M. Hill who left Katalla several weeks ago for the Koyukuk. The letter was mailed at Nulato on the Yukon, and bears date, July 25. Concerning the Koyukuk Mr. Hill says: "There is nothing to get excited about in the Koyukuk so far, although everyone I have seen seems to think that the country is all right. I do not think there have been more than one hundred chechakoes who have gone in there so far this season; and I guess there will be only one more steamboat going up there until spring. I saw Mr. Turner of the Northern Commercial company, a few days ago at Fort Gibbon and he told me that he thought the rush would start into the Koyukuk this fall. He seemed to think the country would be good. He had come down from Bettles only a short time before. However I do not look for any big Koyukuk rush before next spring.

"I expect to be in the Koyukuk country for the next four or five weeks, and then take the last boat down the river and go over to Fairbanks for a couple of months, and expect then to go outside by way of Valdez. I will also probably stop at Katalla on the way down.

"I occasionally see an item or two in the Fairbanks papers about Katalla, and am still in hopes that the town will yet turn out all right."

CLEARING OUT THE TUNNEL

The work of clearing the debris from McDonald's coal mine on Bering lake, the result of the explosion in the tunnel last May, is now under way. An air fan has been installed since Mr. McDonald went up to the mine last week. The damage done to the mine by the explosion was more extensive than was anticipated and it will take some little time to put the mine in good shape for operating. George W. Evans, the mining expert of Seattle examined the mine this week.

Katalla residents were still hopeful for growth in 1908. The article *"Shepard Creek is Promising"* announces the return of Judge Britton and Oliver L. Willoughby from coal exploration at nearby Shepard Creek. *Alaska State Historical Library, Juneau. Photograph by Ed Ferrell*

FIRST XMAS TREE IN CATALLA, ALASKA, 1903.

Evans, Phot.

Florence Barrett (17 years old) is the young lady with the light dress, second row, center of the photograph. It is believed the man behind her left shoulder is her father, Martin, and the second woman from her right shoulder is her mother, Florence. Brothers Lawrence (18), and Freddie (11) could be in the photograph, also. *Franklin R. Brenneman Collection, Alaska State Library, Juneau*

Katalla was the seat.[5] Such skills as typewriting and clerical work not only provided a livelihood for Florence in later years, they were beneficial for her future writing career.

With few diversions, people of Katalla made their own entertainment, gathering together in large public groups, or small private parties. Right from the start, Martin opened his newly acquired hall to the public. When announcing a party, Martin said through the *Catalla Drill*, "Don't hesitate and ponder on the question as to whether you would be welcome or not, but come."[6]

The excitement of new mineral discoveries brought another adventurer, Oliver L. Willoughby, to Katalla. This

Florence and a friend cut-up on a winter's day in Katalla. *Franklin R. Brenneman Collection, Alaska State Library, Juneau*

thirty-three-year-old newspaper publisher from Port Townsend, Washington, was sent north by Seattle interests to investigate land and mineral possibilities in the Katalla district.[7] Having learned the area, Oliver often guided potential investors to promising discoveries.[8]

Oliver was the younger half-brother[9] of a well-known Washington State sea captain, Charles L. Willoughby, who sailed to Alaska in 1896.[10] Charles had mined through the Chena area[11] and later settled in Katalla. Both brothers would become well acquainted with the Barretts and play important parts in their lives.

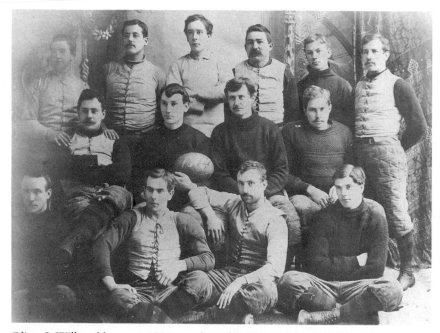

Oliver L. Willoughby was a 1894 member of the Port Townsend Athletic Association. Oliver, about 25 years at the time, is sitting far right in the middle row. *Jefferson County Historical Museum, Port Townsend, Washington*

In a small community like Katalla, it was not strange that permanent residents knew each other well. What attraction drew young Florence Barrett to Oliver Willoughby, who was nearly twice her age, was lost to time. (Could it be that the Willoughby charm had a Martin Barrett flavor?) The two married in Katalla January 24, 1907.[12]

Oliver Willoughby, thirty-eight years old in 1907, was an imposing man. Helen Smith Scudder, who was a young girl in Katalla at the time, recalled this occasion:

> I well remember Ollie Willoughby. He was the tallest man in Katalla. The only law enforcement officer in the town was the U.S.

Commissioner—a man named Brittain. He left Katalla for a short trip to the States. While gone, the gold miners came down from the creeks and started raising hell. The townspeople appointed Dad to fill Judge Brittain's shoes temporarily. Dad picked two men to help him quell the unruly miners—one was Ollie Willoughby because he was the biggest man in town. I remember the three men leaving our home, each with a lantern and Mother and we two children watching them from a window and my poor scared Mother saying, "I hope your Father comes back alive."[13]

Although the two neighboring towns competed for railroad construction during the early 1900s, attention focused on Katalla because of earlier coal and oil discoveries. Eventually the Guggenheim Syndicate—operating as the Alaska Syndicate for this project—decided on Katalla as the port for access to copper country. A railroad would be built there.[14]

Katalla soared to the height of confidence in 1907:

Anywhere from 5,000 to 10,000 persons including construction workers, oil men, coal miners, prospectors, Chinese coolie laborers, Bohunks, Irishmen, card sharps and phony stock brokers, jammed Katalla in 1907. It was probably the most rip-roaring open town since Nome or Dawson, for that year.[15]

Later, when Florence was well known, she told of these times in her interviews. Men of all characters came to her father's saloon and restaurant. In the circle around the stove "are sailors, explorers, engineers, trappers and squaw-men," Willoughby recalled. "They hail from

A few cattle were brought to Katalla in the early 1900s. Here Flo, shortly after her marriage to Oliver, prepares to capture a calf. *Courtesy of Merion Cass Frolich*

Siberia, from the Arctic, from the mysterious and wonderful valley of Ten Thousand Smokes . . . . "[16]

And each man had his own story to tell. One Katalla worker was Robert Stroud[17] who later became "The Birdman of Alcatraz" and who served one of the longest prison sentences in the history of the United States.[18] Such was the unforgettable and unique atmosphere which was commonplace to Florence.

By this time, all the Barretts were busy. Mother Florence ran the general merchandise store.[19] Lawrence, now into his twenties, was off on his own, returning home periodically.[20] The youngest Barrett, Fred, at sixteen sailed south to attend Whitworth College in Washington State.[21] The Katalla Igloo for Pioneers of Alaska was organized in 1907, and Martin became a charter member.[22]

Among all the growth and activity, Oliver and Florence Willoughby set up housekeeping. Oliver, a promoter, plunged into the exploration business and spent time in the bush doing survey and assessment work in addition to operating his lumber business near town. He had a particular interest in coal and oil development.[23] Florence made a home for Oliver on D Street. She occasionally spent time on backwoods hikes and excursions; the ingredients of wilderness and adventure from these jaunts would later flavor some of her written works. Already her inclination was toward the literary. *The Katalla Herald* of February 4, 1908, reported: "Mrs. O. L. Willoughby entertained a number of ladies on Tuesday afternoon. An impromptu musical and literary program was rendered . . . . "[24]

A tragic note struck the new Willoughby family when Florence delivered a stillborn son on the Monday afternoon two days before Christmas in 1907,[25] only a few weeks before her first wedding anniversary.[26] She convalesced at the Katalla company hospital.

Florence wanted children but her first pregnancy was her last.[27] Even ten years later in a letter to Ollie the sad-

Florence always spoke of loving the outdoors. Here she and a friend enjoy the beach along the Katalla coast. *Courtesy of Merion Cass Frolich*

ness rings through: in their northern home, Florence was stripping wallpaper in preparation for painting.

> I tore off some of the green paper there and saw the first paper (with the red roses) that we had. . . . And I remembered all the thoughts I used to have in those days. . . . Thoughts about our baby. And the little brackens you went out in the woods to get when we were first married.[28]

Though Florence carried this sadness with her, her zest for life was not diminished. The name of Mrs. O. L. Willoughby was sprinkled through *The Katalla Herald* as one of entertainer and of being entertained.

4

The Winds of Change

The twenty years Florence Barrett lived in Alaska, and more specifically the fifteen she spent in Katalla, bonded her with the northland. She might have remained in the territory, but circumstances—and her own restlessness—combined to move her south. She would carry with her the excitement, the mystique of the wilderness, which she later translated into her writings. There would be a period yet before she relocated, but influences moved in that direction. What was happening in Katalla was but one factor.

The storms that roared through Katalla during 1907-1908 proved the town's undoing. Ships could not dock, could not load or unload.

Emma Davis, who wrote of her 1907 Katalla experience in *The Alaska Sportsman* magazine said:

> Storms were *made* here. I have walked against such strong winds that it was necessary to turn around to breathe. The wind gauge at Katalla at one time recorded 120 miles per hour—and then went out of commission.[1]

Downtown section of Katalla (1905) on Katalla Bay. *Alaska State Historical Library, Juneau*

About eight miles of track had been laid outside Katalla when the Alaska Syndicate decided to move railroad operations to Cordova.[2] Hope remained that another company would take over to further the railroad in order to ship coal and oil.

Perhaps the most telling sign of Katalla's downhill turn was the closing of the town's newspaper. In 1909 *The Katalla Herald* printed its last issue. Soon after, the proprietor, John Strong—who would subsequently become governor of the territory[3]—and his wife sailed stateside, with plans to relocate in Alaska at a later date.[4]

For the next few years, the Barretts and Willoughbys hung on in Katalla. Flo's brother, Lawrence, now in his late twenties, worked for Oliver in his Katalla lumber business.[5] Though no records can be found, it seems Lawrence married and divorced. A second marriage—to a girl named Ella—took place. He wrote Florence in 1913, "I am again with *wife*."[6] Later events hinted Lawrence had an eye for the ladies.

For a while Oliver continued oil and coal survey work in the hills and afterward tried to interest promoters in Washington State, headquartering in Port Townsend.[7] He traveled Outside more frequently and for longer periods. Florence kept the home going in Katalla and served as his business contact up north. As the town population shrank, Florence wrote in one letter to Oliver, "Times are dreadfully dull up here."[8]

Knowing how she felt about her father, it must have been a serious blow to Florence when he died of a heart attack on November 23, 1912.[9] He was sixty-six years old.

As if Martin's death was not saddening enough, it was followed three months later by that of Florence's twenty-one-year-old brother, Fred Barrett. Fred died of tuberculosis early in 1913 in Spokane, Washington.[10]

Yet another change for the Barretts soon followed. Only four months after Fred's death, Martin's widow, Florence Barrett, slipped over to Valdez on the steamship *Sampson* with Charles Willoughby—Oliver's older half-brother—and married him. The ceremony was performed on Saturday afternoon, June 31, 1913, by Judge Shepherd.[11] The newlyweds were comparable in age—she forty-six years old, he fifty-one. This Barrett/Willoughby union made young Florence Willoughby both a daughter and a sister-in-law to her mother.

There was every evidence that young Florence thought highly of her new stepfather. She consulted him on business matters for her husband[12] and listened to the many adventures he experienced in Washington State, Canada, and Alaska. Commenting on Charles' death years later, *The Alaska Weekly* of Seattle stated:

> Many of Barrett Willoughby's most popular
> stories are founded on the colorful incidents of
> her stepfather's life. He was ever keenly inter-
> ested in her literary efforts and would spend
> hours with her, backtracking over half forgot-
> ten trails, and calling to mind days of wild ad-
> venture in the North.[13]

One of Barrett Willoughby's books *(Alaskans All)* was dedicated to her stepfather, Charles.

By late 1913, Florence's brother Lawrence and his wife Ella announced they were going to have a baby. Florence was elated, and in her own mind she named the Barrett-to-be "Frederick Martin" after the brother and father who had died. She wrote Ollie:"You know our Fred [meaning her brother] always liked blue the best and some way I'm hoping and thinking we may get him back a little bit in this new baby that is coming to us."[14]

And then, as was sometimes the case with separation, rumors began drifting up to Florence that Oliver was "skylarking around with ladies."[15]

Instead of hurt and indignation, Florence answered with some of the spunk, which later held her in good stead during rougher times:"If I were a clinging vine instead of a fighter you would have hated me long ago."[16]

In spite of the rumors and the cooling of the relationship through distance, Florence addressed her letters to "Dearest husband in the world," and "Dear Ollie-boy," and often called him "Cuddle-boy" and "Angel-Lamb,"— she signing her letters, "Do-da." Florence forgave Ollie almost anything."When you tell me anything it is just the same as if God had spoken, so far as *truth* goes," she said in another letter.[17] Apparently she was proud of him and his

Anniversary letter from Florence in Katalla to Ollie in Port Townsend, January 1914. *Jefferson County Historical Society, Port Townsend, Washington. Photograph by Ed Ferrell*

attraction to females. As turn about, several times in her letters she told Ollie of a few Katalla men showing *her* attention, too.

But there were undercurrents in the letters that boded ill for the marriage. Besides money and distance problems, Florence, for instance, seemed to want to point out Ollie's shortcomings but felt badly about criticizing him. Repeatedly when she did, she ended up blaming herself. "I am only funning. Nobody is nicer and sweeter than you, sometimes, and no one is more hateful and mean than Do-da sometimes."[18]

At that time, with a winter Katalla population of about 150,[19] there were barely enough community activities to keep the town going. When the Charles Willoughbys decided to spend the winter in the south, the town was even more empty for Florence.[20]

By June of 1914, Florence had not seen Oliver for over eleven months.[21] Florence Willoughby's days, even with her family gone, were not idle, however. One diversion was a correspondence course in writing.[22] Though her first recorded sale was a modest one—$.50 for a household hint—it was enough to encourage her.[23] In that same month, she wrote a 500-word article on Indian baskets and sent it off with photographs.[24]

Within the following year, Florence took passage on a ship south and visited Ollie.[25] When she returned with her mother and stepfather in September, she wrote "Everything is just the same as when we left," adding, "except there was some government activity."[26]

Florence Willoughby began writing as a Katalla correspondent for *The All-Alaska Review* which published for two years. She supplied snippets of local information and a few articles for the magazine, sometimes signing her name or initials.[27]

After the few writing sales she had over 1914-1915, including a story in *Boy's World* which sold for $2.50,[28]

An oil derrick in the Katalla area. Oil—along with coal and copper—attracted developers to the southcentral region. Oliver Willoughby was deeply involved in mineral discoveries there. *Barrett Willoughby Photograph Collection, Rasmuson Library, University of Alaska Fairbanks*

THE ALL-ALASKA REVIEW

16

❈ Elias Light is Ready for Busin

(By FLORENCE WILLOUGHBY)

During the week the big light at the Capt St. Elias Light Station will be turned on, marking the practical completion of the most modern and substantial station the government owns in Alaska. Mr. F. J. Dorher, foreman of construction, is in town with most of his crew waiting for a south bound steamer, and reports that the light has already been tested and a small force of mechanics are finishing up the installation of machinery and the adjustment of the light. All that now remains to be done is the grading and terracing of the grounds, which work will be put off until next spring.

An appropriation of $115,000 has been expended on the construction of

the Light Station, which, from point of scenery, beauty and stability of construction, and importance to navigators, will be one of the show places on the Alaska run. Built on the south end of Big Kayak Island in the lea of the Great White Cape known locally as Whitestone, it looks down from an elevation of a hundred feet above the sea, on one of thhe most unique rock formations on the Pacific Coast —Big Stone or Pinnacle Rock, a black fang of the deep, that bares itself 500 feet above the currounding reefs.

Breakers from each side of the Cape come crashing together at this point. In times of storm, making such another boiling, roaring, awe-inspiring spectacle as must have inspired Stevenson when he wrote "The Merry Men." It is one of the most dangerous points in the North Pacific.

When the station was planned, the ca Service figured on three years to complete the work, but Mr. Dorher, who loc has had entire charge of construction thi work has achieved the unusual, as h na leaves the work practically finished at U the end of two years—a remarkable Ru record in a country where supplies are so hard to get and to land. st

In excavating for the fog signal an station, Mr. Dorther came upon some cr interesting relics of former days. He an was obliged to cut down a group of d spruce trees, which were thirty-five ar feet in height. After taking out the be roots and digging down for ten feet, m he came upon a large iron hoop im wi bedded in the clay formation. It was ac heavier than any hoop of this period. tr It measured over three inches in ed width. He also found a silver ring, ha evidently beaten out by hand, and bu not connected in the back, as is the th

One of Florence Willoughby's first published articles appeared in the September/ October 1916 issue of the *All-Alaska Review. Alaska State Historical Library, Juneau*

Florence found her success had whipped Katalla into a literary frenzy. She wrote Ol, "The divine gift of literary criticism has descended on half the community. The other half has taken to writing articles."[29]

Sunset Magazine proved the vehicle that gave Florence Willoughby a broader national exposure. In the first half of 1916 alone, *Sunset* published three Alaskan articles by Florence under their feature, "Interesting Westerners." They featured George Watkins Evans,[30] the authority on coal; Alice Anderson, nurse and teacher;[31] and George Barrett, one of the discoverers of the Katalla coal fields.[32]

Other communities near Katalla took notice. When Florence sailed to Seward, the *Seward Gateway* published a few lines about her visit. The article was reprinted in Cordova by *The Alaska Times*:

ACCOMPLISHED KATALLA LADY
VISITING SEWARD FRIENDS

Mrs. Frances [sic] B. Willoughby, of Katalla,
arrived to spend a few days visiting Seward, and
she is the guest of Mrs. Harry Halderston. Mrs.
Willoughby is a clever writer, whose work ap-
pears often in outside publications. She has a
very successful future ahead if she continues the
work (*Seward Gateway*).[33]

The year 1917, however, was not a good one for
Florence. Writing sales proved one of the only encour-
agements.

As the writing successes increased, the marriage with
Oliver deteriorated. After another period of separation—
Florence in Katalla, Oliver in Port Townsend, Washington—he filed for divorce on the grounds that Florence
"deserted and abandoned" him. The judgment was
granted on April 16, 1917.[34]

There did not appear to be many assets from the marriage. This did not bother Florence. She wrote:

I know you can't send me any money, Ollie.
I haven't asked you for any. It's all right. I'm
getting along very well and I feel very good
now—so don't you worry about me.[35]

Although legally the marriage was broken, a bond remained between Florence and Oliver. Both kept up correspondence, Florence still signing her letters with the
affectionate "Do-da." In the end, it was the name
"Willoughby" along with her maiden name of "Barrett"
that she used as her author's pen name.

These were times of World War I, of changes in the
world. Some of Florence's letters to Oliver reflected a

restlessness in her. A thirty-year-old divorcee, she wrote of becoming a war nurse or of traveling to South America with her friend, author Katherine Wilson.[36] Katalla was the longest residence she had known, and it was becoming a ghost town. Divorced from Oliver, she was no longer needed as a business contact up north. He was heavily involved in coal claim problems[37] and did not have money to give her. The senior Willoughbys were the strong ties that kept her rooted in Katalla. She had to earn her own living, and Katalla did not look bright for business opportunities.

Perhaps all these factors, along with an irrepressibly romantic nature, combined to launch Florence into an impulsive second marriage. Only two and a half months after her divorce, Florence ran off from Katalla with one of Oliver's former coal employees then living in Anchorage—Roger Summy. Her new husband was Minnesota born and a year younger than Florence.[38] Romantically enough, they were married "on the high seas" on a ship out of Valdez, Alaska, on the fourth of July, 1917.[39] However, according to the terms of the Willoughby divorce, neither Florence nor Oliver were to contract a new marriage within six months of the decree. Hence, the Summy marriage was illegal.[40]

Roger had worked around Katalla for years. Former Katalla resident, Helen Smith Scudder, remembered him as "a good looking fellow around town."[41] She went on to say Florence did not know he had become a heavy drinker, and that may have been a major reason for their subsequent divorce. "He rushed me into it [marriage]," she told Ollie.[42] Before that disillusion set in, Florence moved to the growing town of Anchorage to be with her new husband.

Brother Lawrence Barrett and his family lived in Anchorage, too, but not for long. In the fall, the Barretts took off for the oil boomtown of Casper, Wyoming.

Hiking in the mountains afforded pensive time for Florence ("Barrett") Willoughby.
Courtesy of Merion Cass Frolich

Following closely behind—presumably hot on the trail—was Lawrence's friend, "Seattle Bessie" Fisher. In Casper, after a week of heated arguments, Bessie shot Lawrence while the Barrett family ate at the Rhinoceros restaurant on October 26, 1917. Lawrence died the next day.[43]

Lawrence's mother, the senior Florence, was visiting her sister in Berlin, Wisconsin, at the time of the shooting and took the first train west to Casper.[44] She and Lawrence's wife transported his body to Port Townsend, Washington, for burial.[45] Now, the future Barrett Willoughby had already lost her other brother; mother Florence and a three-year-old niece were the only relatives left in her immediate family.

While in Anchorage as Mrs. Summy, Florence continued to write to her former husband, Ollie. In an April 17, 1918, letter she mentioned she was taking a course of some kind, "I go to school every morning . . . ." The tone of the letter suggests she was not happy. "Roger rushed me into it [marriage], and is impatient," "Roger is gone always," "I never even have a meal with him . . . ." She talked of going home to Katalla and of going Outside to Washington State.[46]

Florence soon decided the marriage to Roger was a mistake. She returned to Katalla, separated from Summy, the following May of 1918.

"I was so glad to leave Anchorage that I executed a dance (with a suitable partner) on the stern of the old *Alameda* for sheer joy," she wrote Ollie.[47]

While in Katalla, Florence considered options before making another decision. For one, she was concerned about her mother. She told Oliver in the same letter:

> Mother doesn't laugh much anymore. She just sits—with her hands folded and looks off into space. That is why I want to get her away from here . . . Katalla seems the end of the

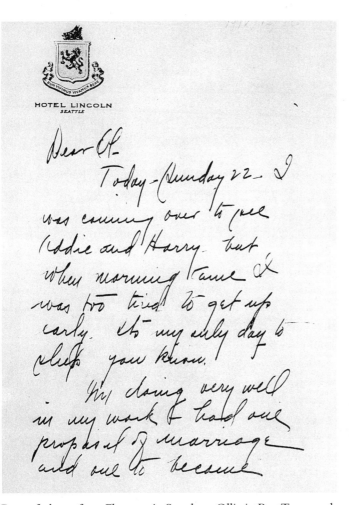

Page of a letter from Florence in Seattle to Ollie in Port Townsend, December 1918. *Jefferson County Historical Society, Port Townsend, Washington. Photograph by Ed Ferrell*

world now that we have but one boat a month.
I wish mother would get Charley away from
here. She is very anxious to go, but he seems
perfectly contented.[48]

In spite of concern about leaving her mother in Katalla,
Florence decided to move south "and find a market for
my dreams."[49] She made a permanent change that summer. By October 1918 Florence wrote Ollie to tell him
that she was staying in a private home in Tacoma,
Washington, and going to school.[50] Whitworth College
did not have records of that time, but it was believed Florence enrolled there; her brother Fred had been a student
at Whitworth ten years earlier.

Studying kept her busy, but writing was still on her
mind. Her author friend, Katherine Wilson, said she had
the "gift of writing" and encouraged her to move to San
Francisco.[51]

Florence made a quick trip to Seattle in October for
the final Summy divorce decree and happily closed the
chapter on that part of her life.[52]

Two failed marriages disillusioned Florence and made
her "sick at heart," which she admitted to Ollie.[53] Apparently she had a strong need to be loved and sought after,
and she wanted others to be attracted to her. "[I] had one
proposal of marriage, and one to become a mistress . . . I
have to laugh," she wrote Ollie from Seattle.[54]

By February 1919, Florence worked for a Tacoma law
firm—Grosscup & Morrow. As spring returned, she became lonesome for Katalla. Paying her divorce bill, or her
"alimony" as she called it, kept her on the job.[55]

Still the writer at heart, Florence finally made the move
to San Francisco and was settled on Bush Street by January 1920.[56] It was there she decided to write in earnest.

5

A First Romantic Novel

San Francisco, with its cultural activities, sophistication, and weather agreed with Florence Willoughby. She later admitted San Francisco "is the only city that I love."[1] California was a total change from Katalla but just what she needed. She felt "frisky" and "full of story plots."[2] Though there was no evidence she sold articles while in Tacoma, she kept writing. *Sunset Magazine* published more of her articles in February 1921, February and April of 1923, and May 1926.

Occasionally Ollie[3] sent her a little money to help keep her going. He also arranged for her to receive copies of Washington and Alaska newspapers. Keeping in touch with the north country was important to her.[4]

A few months in San Francisco and Florence obtained a secretarial job with author/reviewer Frederick O'Brien. Excitement now showed through in her letters. Frederick O'Brien (Irish, and fanciful—again like Martin Barrett?) surrounded himself with literary people of the day such as Fanny Hurst, Edna Ferber, Lowell Mellett, and Irving Cobb.[5] O'Brien offered Florence helpful advice which she followed daily in her writing. He said, "Be yourself and keep a diary."[6] She did both.

With her first paycheck, Florence did an extremely "Willoughby" thing: she spent money on something extravagant to lift her morale.

> I bought a lot of silk underwear the first thing. It feels fine next to my skin, and now I will try and get some outside clothes, and look decent again. There are so many places to go here, and I have many invitations as men seem to like me, but I do not go on account of not feeling well dressed, but now, doggone it, I can get some raiment for festive occasions.[7]

Helen Smith Scudder said the same thing. "[O]ne time low on funds, Florence spent all she had on some lovely perfume to raise her spirits."[8]

Willoughby kept an exhausting routine, working and then continuing her own writing about five hours a day.[9] But she felt encouraged and happy.

When her book *Where the Sun Swings North* was completed, Florence Willoughby wrote Rockwell Kent. She had read Kent's illustrated book about Alaska, *Wilderness*, and said it made her yearn for Alaska. Kent forwarded Willoughby's letter to his publisher, George Palmer Putnam. Intrigued, Putnam wrote Willoughby asking to see some of her work.[10] Florence sent him a copy of *Where the Sun Swings North* and Putnam published it in 1922.

The novel is a fictionalized account of her family's experience while marooned on Middleton Island. It includes an Indian antagonist and a romance, as the family struggled to survive. In this novel, Willoughby roughly formed the cast of characters she would employ through most of her fiction. The group normally included an idealized heroine, a bad-girl foil, rival loves, an Irish father, a housekeeper, and a male California connection. There were variations on these characters among the books, but nothing extreme.

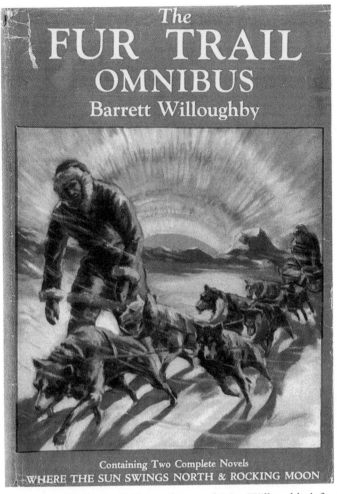

Dust jacket of *The Fur Trail Omnibus*, combining Willoughby's first two novels, *Where the Sun Swings North* and *Rocking Moon*, 1925. *Courtesy of Joan Buhler, Port Townsend, Washington*

Where the Sun Swings North, printed under the pen name of Barrett Willoughby, proved the first in numerous successes which brought her national attention and some international notice.[11] The book was dedicated to her mother, "who can make a tent in the wilderness seem like home." Before coming out in book form, the story ran serially in *The Chicago Tribune*.[12]

From the first time Florence used the pen name of Barrett Willoughby, at least in part following her publishers advice to take a man's name for her work,[13] there was confusion over her gender. People who wrote her letters addressed them to "Mr. Willoughby."[14]

The subjects of her books and the—for those days—rugged vocabulary all suggested a man's writing. A reviewer friend noted:

> The reference of Barrett Willoughby as "she" will astonish many readers. Her book is so virile. She is one of the few, the very few women writers who can evoke a real man between the pages of a book.[15]

Because of the masculine connotation of her name, and the naturalness of her male characters, one critic mistook author for character. Another reviewer of *Where the Sun Swings North* wrote: "This man Willoughby has evidently released his own inhibited ruthlessness by writing himself into the masterly and brutal villain of the book."[16]

Florence was fond of saying in interviews:

> Before I was ten, I was proficient in the use of man phrases—scientific, adventurous, poetic and profane. My French teacher in the convent where I was educated used to through [sic] up her hands and say: "o-o-o! This Alaskan child! Such infelicity of language." But later, after I

became a writer, I thought myself very lucky
to have learned how real men talk.[17]

Florence lashed out when people dubbed her a
"he-man."

> I feel about as sexless as a figure in a totem
> pole. . . . Please if you should review my book,
> don't call me a He-man! It is true I'm an
> Alaskan . . . but I'm only five feet two inches
> tall, and I'm mighty glad to be just a little
> woman.[18]

She was, in fact, proud of her femininity. From the
start Willoughby was intensely interested in being feminine and in being attractive to men. "I seldom wear trou-
sers when roughing it," she assured a radio audience,

> first because they feel stiff and uncomfortable—
> and I've yet to see a woman in trousers who
> looks well from the rear! Second, I don't wear
> them because Alaska men like their women in
> skirts—and I can always get better stories from
> them when I wear skirts. I have never wished I
> were a man instead of a woman.[19]

Early censure came from a literary critic examining one
of her manuscripts. Willoughby related what he told her:

> Jack London and Rex Beach had written
> Alaska completely out. And that I was very
> crude and unladylike in my expressions—I
> believe he used the term "ribald"—and that I
> must study the ways of refined, civilized people
> before I could hope to succeed.[20]

Frederick O'Brien, her first real literary employer and teacher, set her straight. He told her to call it like it was. Be yourself, he said. Suit the words to the subject. When she fashioned her Alaskan scenes into ladylike molds, he censured her. "Woman words," he scolded. "Bah! That's the trouble with all women writers—they smother their meaning in adjectives and saccharine phrases! . . . Woman words—cut out the woman words."[21]

In spite of the masculine association, Florence took pride in the wilderness background which set her apart from other women, and other women writers. So many of the experiences she wrote about were, after all, masculine in focus. For her day and subject, she was unique.

It was at this point in her life that Willoughby began the Alaska commute. Just as she had done in earlier years for school and trips—traveling from Alaska to the States—she continued the pattern, in reverse, for her books. While she headquartered and wrote in San Francisco most of the year, when Florence needed raw material, she sailed to Alaska. Telling a reporter of her numerous journeys north, she said:

> I see myself now lying in the sun in a top deck chair as my steamer moves north through the quiet river-like waterway of Alaska's inland sea. On one side, so close I can almost touch it with a golf club the shore finged [sic] with cedars, wild roses, wild violets. On the other side . . . a hanging glacier that looks like a frosted sapphire.[22]

Notice of her arrival in the territory was seen in different Alaskan newspapers at various times, depending on which area was the focus of her research:

After the Willoughbys—Charles and the elder Florence—moved from Katalla to California, Barrett's mother often accompanied her author daughter on many Alaskan research trips. Here are Barrett and her mother with three unidentified men, probably outside Sitka or Ketchikan. *Barrett Willoughby Photograph Collection, Rasmuson Library, University of Alaska Fairbanks*

Noted Writer Visits Sitka After Data

Frances Barret [sic] Willoughby, noted writer, sourdough and Alaskan musher spent the past week visiting Sitka gathering material for an all Alaskan novel. . . .

Leaving on the steamer *Queen*, Mrs. Willoughby and her friend are now on their way to Kodiak where they plan to remain for two months or more, gathering information on fox farming, fishing, and other northern industries.[23]

Material gathered by this Kodiak trip would be the basis for her next romantic novel, *Rocking Moon*, which was published in 1925. And then again:

NOTED ALASKA WRITER VISITS WRANGELL

Barrett Willoughby, accompanied by her mother, Mrs. Charles Willoughby, arrived from San Francisco on the Admiral Rogers Monday morning. . . . Her present visit is for the purpose of securing data for further exploiting northern life in both fact and fiction. . . . Miss Willoughby states that Wrangell will have a prominent place in the forthcoming book. . . . [24]

The commuting was necessary, Florence explained, because she needed to stand back from the material. *The Daily Alaska Empire* interviewed her, and the clipping reported:

Barrett Willoughby has a home in San Carlos, California, and a studio in San Francisco. She stated here today that she would live in Alaska permanently were it not that she finds she can't write of Alaska at such short range; she needs to be further away to obtain a proper perspective on her subject matter.[25]

Barrett Willoughby further reported she needed this travel for inspiration. During another interview, she stated:

Outside of keeping a diary, I never do any writing in Alaska. Up there I'm too busy and

Fishing was one of the Alaskan activities Barrett Willoughby enjoyed
when she traveled north. *Courtesy of Merion Cass Frolich*

too happy just living. When I can put it off no
longer, I come down to my California home
and start my new book. When in Alaska I roam
from one shore to the other. Last year I
covered six thousand miles in two months, up
there, using steamers, railroads, cruisers, canoes,
automobiles and airplanes. . . . Every time I fin-
ish a novel, I go back home and jaunt around
up there until financial necessity forced me to
begin another book. I'm notoriously improvi-
dent, impractical, impromptu and, some say,
improper.[26]

But wasn't traveling in a wild country like Alaska
uncomfortable, an interviewer asked? And wasn't it dangerous? Willoughby responded:

The real Alaskan does not encounter many
hardships—he uses his brains to avoid them;
neither does he indulge in unnecessary hero-
ics. It's the cheechako [a newcomer to the north]
who has such a terrific time up there. And even
he must be mighty foolhardy to encounter gru-
eling hardships in a land accessible at every point
by airplane.[27]

Actually experiencing events was important to
Willoughby. She used her enthusiasm and her senses to
absorb the feel of locations, and she was skillful enough to
later translate those experiences onto the printed page.

For instance, Florence did not want to imagine and
then write vicariously about riding in an airplane—she
wanted to fly; if a certain risk was involved, it only sharp-
ened the experience.

Carol Beery Davis of Juneau remembered taking
Willoughby on an outing to Admiralty Island aboard the
Davis family's cruiser. The Davises had intended to feed

Florence breakfast on the boat, but she had already eaten and was assigned the wheel while everyone else ate. When breakfast was over, Willoughby did not want to give up the wheel. She enjoyed handling the boat and steering her own course.[28]

Mrs. Davis further recalled that Willoughby would put on any kind of clothing—riding pants, goggles, gown, fishing boots, etc.—in order to live a new experience.[29] No armchair writer was Barrett Willoughby.

Once *Where the Sun Swings North* was published, reviewers found it refreshing at least to evaluate an Alaskan book written by someone who had lived in the territory. The book rang true because the author had actually experienced the ordeal of being marooned on an island. One reviewer stated:

> The plot is pure melodrama, even to the dear old indispensable scene of the villain chasing the fair lady round the room, and the hero turning out to be the son of the president of the Alaska Fur and Trading Company, in disguise. But the superimposed details and descriptions of life in Alaska make a book worth reading even by those whose eyelids are a little weary when it comes to watching the villain still pursue her.[30]

Alaskan reaction to the book was positive. No sooner had the novel reached northern bookstores than *The Sitka Tribune* reported:

> Sitka people that have read "Where The Sun Swings North," the new book by Florence Willoughby who was in Sitka last summer, says ti [sic] breathes the real Alaskan spirit. It is interesting and clean, like the great out-of-door in the Northland.[31]

The Pathfinder

A REAL ALASKAN NOVELIST

Mrs. Florence Willoughby, from early childhood a resident of Alaska, the latest Alaskan novelist, will spend he summer at Kodiak gathering material for a new Alaskan novel.

Mrs. Willoughby writes under the pen name of Barrett Willoughby, and her first book, "Where the Sun Swings North," is now running as a serial in the Chicago Tribune. It will come from the press in book form in October. The publishers are Putnam's Sons, of New York.

"Where the Sun Swings North" is a story of Alaskan life, and the greater part of the action takes place on Middleton, that lonely spot sixty miles south of the entrance to Prince William Sound, during the days of the old Alaska Commercial Company, and it is based on facts.

It is claimed that Barrett Willoughby is the first real Alaskan novelist, as she has been in the country since she was si xyears old. Her father, Martin Barrett, adventurer and prospector, came to Alaska in his own schooner, cruising along the entire coast of Alaska, and bringing his family with him. For many years he was a resident of Katalla.

"Scotty" Allen, who read "Where the Sun Swings North" in the manuscript, says: "It is so true to the country about which it is written that even an Alaskan can read it and enjoy it."

For the last three years Mrs. Willoughby has been in San Francisco, where she was employed as private secretary to Frederick O'Brien, the famous writer of South Sea stories. Her occupation has brought her in contact with the large lights in the famous Pacific Coast center center of art and literature.

Mrs. Willoughby is young, pretty, and in love with her work and enthusiastic.

Miss Blue Jay

By R. S. Dodge

My little girl friend was here to-day,
Looking so happy, pert and gay,
Dressed in her best, as fashions go,
Almost perfect from head to toe.

She had on a skirt of a beautiful blue,
With a shirtwaist of a different hue;
A jet-black toque upon her head
Shot through with a golden thread.

Her shoes were black, with pointed toes;
But I was shocked, for she wore no hose.
She gave me a look of cold, black scorn:
Dear sir, I have worn none since I was born.
I have looked over the wash on the family tree,
And I wear what nature gave to me.

SHIP YOUR FURS TO

SEATTLE FUR SALES AGENCY

FLYNN BROS.

We are old Alaskans and know how to get the highest prices for your furs.
We have the keenest competition. Try us.

SEATTLE, WASH.

Valdez Sheet Metal Works

VALDEZ, ALASKA

FRED COLECLOUGH, Prop.

STOVES,	AIR PIPE
RANGES,	HOSE
PLUMBING	VALVES
HEATING	FITTINGS
HARDWARE	SHIP CHANDLERY
PAINTS	OILS

MOTOR BOAT SUPPLIES.   REPAIRS OF ALL KINDS.

If it is made of metal we have it.

Agents for Frisco Standard Gas Engine and Kaustine Products.

ERLAND & CO., INC.

E. ERLAND

SAIL MAKERS AND RIGGERS
CANVAS GOODS

MARITIME BLDG.   SEATTLE. WASH.

C. M. LAMPSON & COMPANY

LONDON,   ENGLAND.

PUBLIC AUCTION SALES OF
RAW FURS

Represented by   212 Fifth Ave.
ALFRED FRASER   NEW YORK

ROOMS WITH BATH   ROOMS EN SUITE

STEAM HEATED

HOTEL PARSONS

BEST FURNISHED HOTEL IN ALASKA
UP-TO-DATE IN EVERY RESPECT

ANCHORAGE   ALASKA

When writing to Advertisers mention The Pathfinder

Alaska's magazine, *The Pathfinder*, was one of the media sources to proclaim Barrett Willoughby the first real Alaskan novelist, as in this May 1922 issue. *Alaska State Historical Library, Juneau. Photograph by Ed Ferrell*

The Pathfinder of February 1923 followed with:

> [T]he story is truer to Alaska and its people than
> any novel that has yet been published—and it
> is also artful, so artful that it is a delightfully
> fascinating story.[32]

Barrett Willoughby's personal life brought a change
during the mid-1920s. Her stepfather, Charles—then in
his sixties—finally gave up on Katalla, whose population
had dropped to about fifty.[33] Charles and the senior
Florence relocated to California and moved in with Barrett
Willoughby.[34]

6

Building a Reputation

B y the mid-1920s, Florence had fashioned a biography of herself and how she began writing. She
used this history—with slight variations—in subsequent
public interviews through the years.

For the most part the account was true, but Florence was a
storyteller first and a historian second. Her version was a romantic one and not entirely factual.

In the first place, Willoughby was older than she led people to
believe. And in the second place, she was not born in Alaska, but
gave that impression. Third, after World War I, German ancestry
was not a popular lineage; though her mother had been born in
Germany, in interviews Florence introduced her as being a "blond,
English lady."[1]

Barrett Willoughby was an intelligent woman, and she gave
her audiences what they wanted. When she answered the question, "How did you begin writing," this was generally how she
replied:

> I am an Alaskan and a writer—a storyteller. That's
> really a natural enough combination. Nearly every-
> one in my country *is* a storyteller because we have to

depend so much on ourselves for amusement up there during the long winter nights. At my home, in a little out-of-the way village on the Alaskan coast, my father keeps a trading post. Our big, ramshackle store is really a sort of wilderness club. On winter nights, the men gather and form a circle about the big stove made of a gasoline drum. . . . Everyone of them is an adventurer and everyone has a tale to tell. I know because I always used to wedge myself into a dark corner by the sugar barrel to listen, and watch them through the haze of their tobacco smoke. And marvelous yarns they tell, those Sourdoughs, tilting back in their chairs, their mackinaw coats unbuttoned, their caps pushed back on their heads. Those old friends gave me my first lessons in the art of fiction![2]

This Katalla background sounded as if Florence were a young child at the time, while actually she was in her late teens.

Perhaps Florence can be forgiven for smoothing the edges of her early history for the basics were fact: she had spent her youth in Alaska; she had lived an exciting life in unusual places; she had met fascinating and unique people; and she did love Alaska. Willoughby understood Alaska and Alaskans because she had lived there. What was far-off adventure to the average American had been everyday life to Florence.

The *Ketchikan Alaska Chronicle*, for one, awarded her Alaskan standing:

It is said of her by old-time Alaskans that she is the only author of Alaskan stories who has ever captured the elusive and real twang of the north in the "atmosphere" of her stories.[3]

When people asked about publishing her first piece, Florence again gave the general facts in a romantic and amusing fashion:

> I broke into print accidently while I was in the States. . . . Being overcome with homesickness I sat down one night and wrote a little sketch of my home town. I was so taken with the appealing qualities of my townspeople—as I had depicted them—I wanted the whole world to know the dear folks, so I sent the sketch to a magazine. It was accepted and published.
>
> Being still in the States I waited eagerly for letters telling me how proud they all were of me. The first one came from my mother. She wrote:
>
> "Dear Daughter: Everyone here is reading your piece in the magazine. Perhaps it would be better if you would write about a subject outside of your home town. You must remember, dear, we have to make our living here. Your brother has had three fights this week over your article. Your father is paying the hospital bills of Nosey Owen, whom he was obliged to beat up because Nosey criticized your article so severely. . . . "[4]

Her mother's letter went on, but the overall reaction was there, and it was amusing for a general audience to hear. Perhaps her account was not entirely true, but it was presented with a storyteller's license.

If the facts about Willoughby and her activities were sometimes exaggerated or misleading, there was one truth few could quarrel with: Florence was enthusiastic about Alaska.

I determined to write of Alaska as it really is today. A gracious, good-time land, greater in area than the combined countries of England, Ireland, Scotland, Wales, Norway, Sweden, Finland and Denmark; and the whole magnificent stretch from the Pacific to the Arctic Ocean, a garden of wild flowers in summer, alive with birds and fish and game.[5]

Stateside people always had the wrong idea about Alaska as Willoughby stated later in her career:

I get letters from people all over the world who read my books about Alaska. . . . The prevailing idea—born of Dan McGrew and the movies—seems to be that Alaska is a 60 below land of eternal ice and snow and frozen wastes. . . . A land peopled by unshaved ruffians, in parkas, who get roaring drunk on hootch and shoot each other in saloons for the possession of virgin gold and unvirginal females.[6]

Her Alaskan experience was her livelihood, and Willoughby gave every evidence of truly loving and appreciating the territory.

But nothing could keep me from writing about Alaska. I love the place. There's something in the air up there—a sense of expectancy that is the very essense [sic] of youth and romance. When you wake up in the morning—no matter how old you are—you have that feeling you had when a child—"Something wonderful is going to happen today." I knew if I could get that into my writing that people everywhere would like to read my books. . . .[7]

Willoughby waves from a boat in Alaskan waters, 1932. This picture was used as a jacket photo on some of Willoughby's books. *Barrett Willoughby Photograph Collection, California Section, California State Library, Sacramento*

And in a radio talk for NBC on June 6, 1932:

> I want to tell the whole world what a beautiful land it is. A land of bright courage and joyous living, where everybody had an awfully good time.
>
> And when people ask about the terrible cold . . . the lawlessness . . . the cruelty of the country, I admit these conditions do exist, just as they do in New York, in Chicago, in many other sections of the United States. But these are the *unusual* phases of Alaska. As such they have been given undue publicity. They are the ingredients of the so-called "he-man" fiction. It's much easier to build stories on such conditions, and naturally most writers have dwelt on them to the exclusion of the happier and less exciting phases. . . . You'd have exactly the same one-sided presentation of the United States if all writers confined themselves to the gangster activities of Chicago, or the blizzard tragedies of North Dakota.
>
> And I've always resented the fact that comparatively all Alaskan fiction had dealt exclusively with the worst and most unusual phases of the North. Hardships of the outland, the cold, the winter gloom. . . . Of course nearly all Alaskan stories published are written by writers who have never lived there. They merely have passed through. And a surprising lot of northern fiction is written by people who have never even been in the North.[8]

And speaking to an audience about travelogues:

> [W]hen the cameraman decided to bring you back a bit of Alaskan home life—what does he

do? He goes way up into the Arctic and returns with reels of fur-clad Eskimos engaged in winter activities. . . . If Jack London had written just a few stories of summer Alaska, I tell you, the world would have a different and much warmer conception of that country today.[9]

Willoughby did her best to counter Alaska's wintry image and to show that the country was more varied. In addition, Willoughby expressed her love of Alaska through many of her heroines. The character Sondra expressed it briefly in the book *Sondra O'Moore*:

Sondra, on the *Tanya's* afterdeck, was savoring the peculiar exhilaration of the moment. This was Alaska. This was home. No other land offered such contrasting ways of life; such stimulus of adventure always in the offing.[10]

In spite of Alaska's icy image and remote location, statesiders were drawn to the territory's romantic image. "Can you get a husband there," was a frequent question for Willoughby, "one like the men in your stories?" "I know from long observation," Willoughby answered,

that the homeliest old maid—provided she has a sense of humor—can get wed in Alaska if she wants to—and feel herself as glamorously young as the youngest bride. . . . I know that the stodgiest . . . old bachelor shuffles off years and inhibitions and becomes gallant, irresistibly masculine and therefore able to command what he wishes since it's the men who create circumstances in Alaska.[11]

While Willoughby published a few short articles for *Sunset* and *American* magazines in the next few years, her major effort went toward completing a second novel—*Rocking Moon*. Florence's cast of fictional characters for this story were more professionally developed when compared with those in her first book. She had shaped the personalities into the roles they would play in subsequent novels. Once *Rocking Moon* was finished, Putnam's published it in 1925.

This second book, a romantic story set in Kodiak, was an immediate success; it was reprinted three times in April, the month it came out, and was in its fifth printing by September of the same year.[12] Seattle *Alaska Weekly* editor, Earle Knight, called Willoughby a "genius."[13] Much of the information for *Rocking Moon* was gathered on a trip to Kodiak Island during the summer of 1922.[14]

The story itself focused on the fox farm industry. Such farms raised foxes and sold their pelts for substantial profits. Add to that setting raiding pirates, love conflicts, a rich Russian background, and an adventurous romance.

Russian history excited Willoughby. She waxed enthusiastic about Kodiak and its people—their varied pasts, their hospitality, the setting in which they lived. At the end of her 1922 visit, she expressed a premonition—perhaps one shared by others who envisioned change:

> It is like living in a delightful, old-world fairy tale to be here, and yet as I stood by the oldest bell in Alaska, looking down on the wharf below the trading post . . . I felt a pang of—was it apprehension? The gas Blazer was loading a dozen horses on her afterdeck. Tanned, open-shirted dock hands and slim khaki-clad engineers were getting ready outfits. Two prosperous, well-fed appearing individuals to [sic] smart city clothes watched these efforts with a patronizing, yet proprietary interest, shifting their cigars from one side of their mouths to

the other. They were getting ready to go to the new oil fields at Cold Bay. They are the fore-runners of big business.

Suddenly I was thankful that I had come in time to see tranquil old Kodiak in her present beauty and charm, before the hustle and bustle of an oil boom descends upon her.[15]

Willoughby dealt with the uneasiness of change in her Irish/Russian character, Nicholas Nash. It was not com-mercial change which bothered Nick but ethnic change. He saw the flavor of Alaska transforming through its people. Nick spoke to this change in one scene with Sasha:

Have you ever thought, Sasha, how the old Russian families are dying out? . . . Ours is the blood that discovered and tamed Alaska, the wildest, most beautiful, most hazardous land in the world! Do we want that blood diluted, lost through marriage with milk-and-water strang-ers from the South?[16]

Kodiak was rich in Russian tradition. A reviewer said:

Tenderly, lovingly, Barrett Willoughby picked up bits of legend and history and wove them into the background of her novel. A Rus-sian, had he attempted to do that, would have lost himself in the part, and forgotten about the new American culture and its influence on modern Alaska. . . .

The "melting pot" [of people] is an absorb-ing theme in itself, the more so in Alaska, where old world influences still survive much and sometimes blundering "Americanization."[17]

Sasha (played by Lillian Tashman) points out the beauty of her blue foxes to Nicholas (Rockcliffe Fellows) during the movie shooting of Willoughby's book, *Rocking Moon*, in the Sitka area. *Barrett Willoughby Photograph Collection, Rasmuson Library, University of Alaska Fairbanks*

It was the vivid descriptions of Russian influence that helped to document a period of Alaskan life. To that date, no other fiction author of Willoughby's stature had done that.

The book itself was dedicated to a Russian priest Willoughby admired—Father Andrew Peter Kashevaroff.

In 1925, *Rocking Moon* was made into a movie. In fact, it was the first time a major Hollywood studio—Metropolitan—filmed on location in Alaska. The studio chose Sitka, rather than Kodiak, to shoot the scenes.

The first big motion picture company from Hollywood to film scenes in Alaska arrived in Sitka on the *Virginia* today, where they will spend three weeks making scenes for "Rocking Moon," a romance of the land of long shadows, on the actuat [sic] locations of the story.[18]

The crew and cast traveled to the Sitka area and filmed at a fox farm outside town. Principals of the film were Lillian Tachman who played the romantic lead and John Bowers who starred as the hero.[19]

Barrett Willoughby met the film crew and stars in Los Angeles before the trip but did not accompany them to Alaska or oversee the filming.[20] When asked if the studio might change the story too much in filming, she was resigned to the fact that might happen.

> I just wrote a story of the Alaska that I know and love. No thought was given to "movie-angle" when a well-known Hollywood company acquired the picture rights to my book. I said to myself with a sigh: let them mutilate it![21]

Both of Willoughby's first two books caused enough sensation to make it worthwhile for publisher Grosset and Dunlap to print *The Fur Trail Omnibus* in 1925. The omnibus included both *Where the Sun Swings North* and *Rocking Moon*.

After *Rocking Moon's* arrival, Willoughby continued writing for *Sunset* and *American* magazines. A number of the articles were later included in a nonfiction volume entitled *Gentlemen Unafraid*, printed by G. P. Putnam's Sons in 1928. Willoughby turned designer for this volume:

> Wishing that even the cover of her new book should express the joyous spirit of Alaska's pioneering adventurers, Barrett Willoughby, the

Barrett Willoughby (center) discusses Alaskan relics with movie stars Laska Winters and Rockcliffe Fellows. The two actors played major parts in the movie version of Willoughby's novel, *Rocking Moon*. *Barrett Willoughby Photograph Collection, Rasmuson Library, University of Alaska Fairbanks*

novelist, designed it herself. . . . The bright but harmonious colors used by the Alaskan Indians, the Thlingets, have been borrowed by the author-designer to express the mood of her book.[22]

Willoughby's first nonfiction book highlighted lives of noteworthy Alaskan men such as her father Martin Barrett; steamboat captain Sydney Barrington; trail blazer Alexander "Sandy" Smith; dog sled racer Scotty Allan; coal field authority George Evans; and plant expert C. C. Georgeson. Willoughby used her storytelling techniques to build suspense and to quicken the pace while dealing with nonfiction material. The book was packed with interesting facts and was written in a readable manner. Consider the ingenuity of Sandy Smith:

> I was up in the Barrens once when the ice went out of the river, leaving me in a country where there wasn't a tree or a piece of timber for hundreds of miles, and where travel on foot was impossible on account of the spongy tundra. But I ripped open some hair seal pelts I had and laced them over my sled, using it as a frame. The craft that resulted wasn't any too roomy or safe, I'll admit; but it floated me down to where I could get a real boat.[23]

For a nonfiction endeavor, *Gentlemen Unafraid* proved weak on dates and documentation; there was no index, bibliography, or notes. The contribution was in the activities of the central personalities and the Alaskan backgrounds in which they operated. The national Daughters of the American Revolution claimed the book was "one of the two greatest books in recent years. . . ."[24]

Not only did Willoughby relate Alaskan times in her nonfiction texts, but she brought those words to instant life through her photographs. *Gentlemen Unafraid* included more than seventy-five black and white pictures of the people and activities on which she focused. Photographs strengthened all her nonfiction works.

The writing going well and her reputation established, Willoughby made another change in her life. After ten years of remaining single, she took the matrimonial plunge once again.

On October 19, 1927,[25] Florence married Robert H. Prosser, a University of California engineer.[26] Robert was eight years younger than Florence; he was born on June

Part scientist part explorer, Sandy Smith was one of Willoughby's subjects in *Gentlemen Unafraid*. Here Smith has fashioned a skiboat to cover the icy snow crust more quickly. *Barrett Willoughby Photograph Collection, Rasmuson Library, University of Alaska Fairbanks*

23, 1894, in Iowa, the son of a Canadian father and an Indiana mother.[27]

People who knew Willoughby said the marriage was a happy one.[28] (Willoughby dedicated *Gentlemen Unafraid* to "Robert H. Prosser, A Gentleman Unafraid.") But the marriage did not last long. While Florence and Robert were on a trip to Philadelphia, Prosser found it necessary to have a sinus operation. He died of complications during surgery on June 9, 1928, two weeks before his thirty-fourth birthday.[29] Whatever married happiness Florence experienced was short lived.

Willoughby submerged herself in work. She wrote the novel *The Trail Eater* which came out in 1929 and was first serialized in *The American Magazine*.[30] What it detailed was best told by Willoughby in the foreward to her book:

> In this novel of love and reckless adventure I tell of the gold town Nome in the heyday of its glory—rich, careless, luxurious, and ugly. . . . I tell of the Sweepstakes Trail, and the daredevil drivers who risked their lives on that four-hundred mile course that is the longest, most hazardous, most cruel—and most fascinating—known to the world of sport.[31]

Florence readily admitted that although the characters were fictional, the racing incidents were drawn from the colorful career of a champion dog sled driver—Allan Alexander Allan. The book was to be made into a California motion picture, but evidently the film never materialized.[32]

Story structure in *The Trail Eater* varied a bit from her standard tale. Willoughby's patterned cast of characters played on scene, but the viewpoint focused more on the hero—Kerry Wayne—rather than on the heroine—Barbee Neilan. The action, too, took place in a wider variety of locations—both inside and outside Nome.

The New York Times called the first half of the book "Frozen North Melodrama" but gave high marks to the ending race itself: "Pages . . . which deal solely with the progress of the race, are intensely vivid and exciting. . . . "[33]

Those particularly—description and action—Willoughby did extremely well. Switching scenes, from Nome to the trail and back again, heightened action and generated page-turning excitement.

While the first edition of *The Trail Eater* was dedicated to "Bob" and Allan Alexander "Scotty" Allan in 1929, this third edition, June 1929, was specifically dedicated "To Bob—On New Trails," after Robert Prosser's death. *Courtesy of Ruth Taylor, Juneau, Alaska*

Following closely on the publication of *The Trail Eater* was *Sitka: Portal to Romance* a year later (1930). This non-fiction work was part travelogue, part romance, and part history; it was a background book rather than a reference.

In conversational style, Barrett Willoughby told her readers of the Russian and Indian influences, their ways, and how they affected life in the historical town of Sitka. She wrote of fur traders, seal hunters, saloon-keepers, Russian ladies—real people. She also spoke of the Russian castle in Sitka and its ruler, Baranov, whom she admired. "I feel, sometimes," she wrote in a letter to friends, "as if I had really lived in those times. What a man he was—that little, level-eyed, Iron Governor!"[34]

Willoughby's *conversational walks* in the book expressed some of her personal beliefs. Take, for instance, her view of life and death when strolling through an old graveyard:

> Here lay empire builders of Mother Russia—gentlemen adventurer . . . fairhaired princess . . . soldier and priest, sea captain and exile. The forest that sprang from their graves was but a fitting symbol of their sturdy souls. . . . Cemeteries are only mournful when they hold the bodies of those whose lives have been uneventful, futile.[35]

Reviewers called it a "chatty book. . . . A good piece of journalism. . . . [It] might well be read by anyone contemplating an inside voyage to South Eastern Alaska."[36]

Hodder Publishers of London, England, printed the book also, under the name of *Sitka: To Know Alaska One Must First Know Sitka.*

A likeness of Baranov's Castle—the Russian influence—was the focal point for the *Sitka* cover. *Photograph by Paul Helmar*

7

A Seasoned Author

Perhaps one of Willoughby's most popular books, and one that best characterized her fiction style, was *Spawn of the North*, published by Triangle Books in 1930. Houghton Mifflin Company and Grosset & Dunlap published it two years later. *Cosmopolitan* magazine purchased and ran *Spawn* as a serial before book publication.[1] So many people bought the novel that the book was in its third printing *before* the actual date of publication.[2]

The topic and the location for the book were the salmon industry in Ketchikan, Alaska. Publicity by *Cosmopolitan* said:

> The swift action takes place during the brief, intense summer season when the salmon surge up from the sea to spawn in their natal streams; when air, water, forests, all are vibrant with the stir of procreation, and when, according to Alaska tradition, men and women, too, go a little mad with love.[3]

The story had plenty of action with fish pirates, weather, and conflicting personal loyalties playing the scenes.

The idea for the book grew with Willoughby from childhood. She stated:

> When I was very small I used to lie spellbound on a log stretched across a stream watching them [salmon] for hours at a time—the threshing, silver mass of salmon fighting their way up to the spawning beds, while eagles and seagulls swooped down upon them to tear out their eyes. I used to think—how terrible—but how wonderful. When I grow up I must write about this.[4]

So when Ray Long, then editor of *Cosmopolitan* asked her to write a good love story of the north, Willoughby thought of fish.

"F-i-s-h!" he said, holding his nose, "Good heavens, you can't mix fish and love successfully."[5]

Willoughby did not agree. She sailed to Ketchikan, finished her research, and after an intense period of writing in California, sent Long the completed story. He read the manuscript and then wrote Willoughby, "Your fish cocktail is perfect—and most potent!"[6]

Willoughby's Alaskan background and personal on-the-scene research brought the story to life and conjured an air of authenticity. "The scenes," *Cosmopolitan* stated, "lend themselves to Barrett Willoughby's fine powers of description." The magazine ended with the statement:

> The author, who has lived this life, has a graphic style which is at its best in a story of deep emotion and exciting adventure. Her love for Alaska, her understanding of its people, and her technical knowledge of the great salmon industry, all contribute to make this book authentic.[7]

Cover photograph of *Spawn of the North*, 1932. *Alaska State Historical Library, Juneau. Photograph by Ed Ferrell*

Research for this book included spending time "down on the waterfront where the seining fleet is moored," Willoughby explained in a radio interview with Ernie Smith, "hobnobbing with the fishermen and sitting in the galley of their little boats drinking coffee and listening to their songs and stories."[8]

Willoughby's fiction relied heavily on plot rather than deep characterization. Nonetheless, there were those readers who found themselves immersed in Florence's characters: "I almost froze to death," remarked a well known English critic after reading a story of hers set against an arctic background.[9]

All her novels were active with excitement, conflict, and romance and were for the most part well written. They evidenced the author's northern background with which many readers were unfamiliar.

In *Spawn of the North* Florence's cast of fictional characters kept the action moving. The book, however, was subtly richer. More defined characters played against each other; the plot proved a bit more complex; there were a few more surprises for the reader; and the heroine was not as idealized as in other books. Though *Spawn of the North* evolved in mid-career for Florence, some might argue that it was her best and most representative work.

A reviewer working for *Booklist* stated:

> Barrett Willoughby brings more to the composition of her west-by-north novel than most of her competitors can summon. A genuine and inborn love of the country puts its unmistakable touch upon her printed enthusiasms. Here is a perfect tale for the movies.[10]

Indeed, the film industry thought it was a good yarn, too. Paramount Studios made the story into a motion picture.

Well-known Hollywood actors such as Henry Fonda, Dorothy Lamour, George Raft, and John Barrymore played roles in the movie version of Willoughby's book *Spawn of the North. Courtesy of the Academy of Motion Picture Arts and Sciences*

It was scheduled for a summer 1936 filming in the Ketchikan area, but the picture was plagued with one obstacle or another. "Bad Luck Dogs Footsteps of Motion Picture Men," reported a *Ketchikan Alaska Chronicle* headline.[11]

The studio planned on Joel McCrea for the male lead, but he had commitments elsewhere.[12] The selected female star, Carole Lombard, became sick.[13] Paramount postponed the picture until, finally, it came out in 1938.[14] In the end, the film studio used Alaskan background scenes in the

A scene from the movie version of Willoughby's book, *Spawn of the North*, starring Henry Fonda, Dorothy Lamour, and George Raft. *Courtesy of Academy of Motion Pictures Arts and Sciences*

picture, but the movie with the cast itself was shot at Lake Tahoe, California.[15] Henry Fonda, Dorothy Lamour, John Barrymore, and Lynne Overman played the principal parts; George Raft was the villainous fish pirate.[16]

Spawn of the North, as well as Willoughby's other novels, were romantic adventures. And therein existed one of the keys to Willoughby's personality and her writing.

If one word depicted Barrett Willoughby as a person and as a writer, it would be "romance." It was the romantic outlook which urged her on, which kept her excited about the future. Her journey in life was like a steamer trip north:

> A warm and magical Alaskan wind that fills me
> with expectancy and makes me sure that
> ahead—up around that next beckoning bend—
> lies something I've always longed for. I don't
> know what it is exactly, but it's beautiful; and it
> has in it youth and buoyancy—and that elusive,
> golden will o' the wisp—Romance.[17]

Romance was a major element in her novels. In *Spawn*,
for example, heroine Dian Turlon's glance met that of a
handsome fisherman and she "caught her breath while
something in her and something in the dark young man
rushed forward, met, and merged in a warm, velvet flood
of light."[18]

Willoughby herself admitted to a thick coating of romantic love. Speaking of her childhood aboard the family
schooner, she later wrote:

> Those are the wild and colorful days that
> tinge all my thoughts of the North. And if my
> presentation of Alaska's history is touched a bit
> with Celtic mysticism and romance, it is be-
> cause my schoolroom was the after-deck of a
> schooner, the teacher my Irish father sitting on
> the water-cask spinning yarns and pointing out
> the places of their happening as we sailed
> along.[19]

The specifics of writing—the plotting, the characterization, the suspense, the pacing—did not come easily to
Willoughby.

When asked what was her greatest joy in writing, she
responded: "I like all of it from gathering the material to
writing it. But I do feel particularly good when I've written a paragraph that makes me feel Alaska."[20]

The "why" of writing came next:

I have an intense love for my country
[Alaska]. . . . I want to offer my readers escape
from conditions that may be harrassing them
here in the States. When I sit down to write I
feel as if I am saying: "Listen, folks, I'm going
to take you on a glorious vacation to my own
land, where everyone has a darned good time
and money doesn't count for much."[21]

Willoughby's diary was by her side constantly while
traveling, and she tried to put down close to 2,000 words
a day to capture the full flavor of her Alaskan location—
everything from storms to landscapes to conversations.[22]

After completing her field research in Alaska, she returned to her California home to write and put the actual
books or articles together.

I write every day from 9 to 4, and it's hard work.
One can't make one's living writing if one waits
for inspiration.[23]

Settled at her desk, Willoughby mulled over the materials and fixed characters and actions in her mind.

[T]hey [characters] stand round in their local-
ity doing nothing. . . . The more I think of
them the more I know about them. . . . Later
on they begin to move. . . . I jot down what
comes to me about them. . . . disconnected
scenes come into my mind.[24]

Once action, plot, and character took form, the story
line could change.

I do not always follow the plot I have out-
lined. When I have gotten into my story and
created the illusion—characters often take the

Tonya

Love for a man she wanted to hate

picture both sides of a chapter in Alaska History that has never
been told before.

Under American rule--no schools. She gathers the creole children
and teaches them. Where?
                    Why Because she thinks it a disgrace thereis
                         no school.

What can grow out of her teaching the kids/?
        The attitude of the American soldiers.
                The idealist
                the rowdy lusting one who steal the golden covers of
                    the bible
                Shenandoah's attitude

At first Tonya tells Shenandoah or Alaska pure. In the end - when she leaves, he tells her.

Tonya: individuality surrounded her like an aura.
s;ert perceptive mind. Quick intuitive soul. Master of forest
and sea lore knew name of every bird, when it came and went and
when and why. Trees, herbage the grasses and rushes of riverside
all interesting to her" the Witch tree--etc.

GET Frame: What the past held, what expects of the future,
            what the present is.

Singing the lament of a Russian lover--see song in Honchraenko stuff

EVERY MOOD OD NATURE her pleasure, rain or shine, storm or calm
she is at one with the elemental forces of the universe. Paraphrased

eyes   heavy-lashed green eyes; Hair brown with dark honey overtones
            skin ivory
            Yonya's leisured world turned topsy turvy.

            sooty black lashes
            long thick sunburned hair
            brown hair the color of maple sugar
            simplicity,honesty the direct approach.

Willoughby took pains in setting up the physical and emotional makeup of
her characters. This is a sample page for a character named "Tonya." *Barrett
Willoughby Photograph Collection, Rasmuson Library, University of Alaska Fairbanks*

action in their own hands, as it were. I [sic]
better situations are evolved than those I have
planned in the beginning. But I like to have a
working plan before I begin the actual writing
of a story. It serves as a springboard for my
imagination.

I begin writing about nine in the morning.
Sometimes I worked only an hour. Sometimes
fourteen or fifteen hours at a stretch. Sometimes I got up in the night and wrote.[25]

Willoughby worked hard at her craft. A close friend,
Herb Hilscher of Anchorage, said of her:

She once told me that she would sometimes
spend an entire day on a paragraph, trying to
phrase the proper mood. . . . Her work does
have mood, and spirit, and the non-mistakable
feeling of early Alaska.[26]

In addition, Willoughby took writing classes. From her
correspondence course twenty years earlier until her death,
she approached a writing project methodically, studying
other authors, reading on a subject. "I'm a slow writer,"
she said, "I lay a strong foundation first."[27]

This foundation consisted of checking libraries to see
what had already been written on a subject, interviewing,
studying the publishing market, researching and outlining
before beginning the actual writing. A newspaper interviewer stated:

Her manner of work is painstaking and thor-
ough—she spent ten months full of eight and
ten-hour workdays on her latest novel. And
after a four days' rest, during which she visited
the libraries and compared notes, she has just

started on a travel book full of interest and unique information. And yet even while she is working on the meaning of a word or the turning of a phrase or calling up some Russian friend to get the correct pronunciation of a name, she never loses sight of the book, or rather of the whole of Alaska behind it.[28]

Hard to please, Florence revised her supposedly finished material endlessly. As journalist and editor Elmer J. "Stroller" White revealed in an interview with Willoughby:

> "Where the Sun Swings North," was rewritten eight times. She spent two years on her last book, "The Trail Eater," and re-wrote it eighteen times.[29]

Since Willoughby worked hard at her craft, she had little patience for those writers who expected her to critique their materials without pay. She said she had received hundreds of manuscripts from unpublished strangers who wanted her to read their books and fix them up so they would sell. In a letter to such an aspiring writer she wrote:

> As one man stated in the note he slyly left in my mail box with his 150,000 word manuscript novel on—fish! "Don't spend too much time on this. Just read it over and add those delicate little touches here and there that make your work so saleable." You see he had been telephoning me every day for a week wanting to bring his manuscript to me—and I had been refusing, because I was working eighteen hours a day trying to finish a serial in time to catch a certain boat for Alaska.[30]

And, conscious of the fact that time was money, she continued:

> I now return all manuscripts from strangers, unopened. One must have time to do one's own writing, you know, or go on relief while one criticizes strangers manuscripts gratis![31]

Once written and with the publisher, her work was not completed. She looked after her material well into the revising stages, too. She was willing to compromise with her editor on certain changes, but at times she insisted on having it her way. The following incident clearly exemplifies the artistic differences between Barrett Willoughby, the independent Alaska woman, and the publishing establishment of that time:

> When I received the galley proofs of my book *Rocking Moon*, I noticed . . . that the language of my characters had . . . been purified. I let it pass until I came to one particular scene. It was where my heroine and her half-breed servant were taking a cruiser through a terrific storm at sea. They were both at the wheel. Suddenly they saw a monster tidal wave rolling toward them—a wave that meant nearly certain death. The half-breed, with his hands clenched, uttered one word: "God!" But when I got my proofs some nice person back in New York had changed that word to the exclamation: "Oh, look!"
>
> That's when I got mad. I wrote a letter to my publisher. I said: "I know from personal experience how men react when they see death coming at them. Their jaws turn the color of a mushroom with fear, and they do not chirp:

"Oh, look!" They gasp "God!" And the word is a prayer.

Well, in a few days I got a reply to my burst of indignation. It was a wire and it read: "Rest easy, Willoughby. God has been reinstated!"[32]

In the end, what was Willoughby's advice to beginning writers?

Before sending stories out to editors, writers should acquire at least a measure of writing technique. . . . For those who have the price, there are some excellent courses by mail; and there are also many reputable private critics. For those who do not have the price, there are the University Extension courses, and the public libraries where innumerable fine text books on writing may be found.[33]

Willoughby's writing methods emphasized hard work and honest craftsmanship. She held to her system for both her novels and her nonfiction.

8

Height of Her Career

F urther research trips to the north country resulted in Willoughby articles published in *The Saturday Evening Post* during the early 1930s. At that time, the *Post* was directed by Quaker interests. One Willoughby article was titled "Volcanoes Packed in Ice," and featured the Jesuit priest Father Bernard Hubbard. After the article appeared, a friend of Willoughby remembered her saying, "It was some feat to get a Catholic priest into a Quaker magazine."[1] The Hubbard article was later included in Willoughby's book *Alaskans All*, which Houghton Mifflin printed in 1933.

Alaskans All was dedicated to Florence's stepfather, Charles. It described the activities of five northlanders: pioneer pilot Carl Ben Eielson; Skagway innkeeper Harriet Pullen; icepilot Louis Lane; priest and geologist Father Bernard Hubbard; and journalist/editor Stroller White.

She met Ben Eielson on a steamer, and he gave her an irresistible invitation, "Come on in to Fairbanks, and I'll fly you around a bit."[2] Fairbanks was off her scheduled route, but Willoughby did not want to miss the opportunity. In those days, flying was still harrowing. There were few airports or highways for emergency landings in the vast, uninhabited country.

Eielson took her up in his open-cockpit biplane. She described the experience as "glorious," until fog threatened them. Nevertheless, flying blind in mountainous country did not dull Willoughby's enthusiasm. She said:

> Ben's manipulation of the plane was such that nothing that may come to me now can ever equal the wild exultation, the sense of cosmic freedom I experienced while he beat about like a trapped bird among the hidden peaks, climbing, side-slipping, banking to avoid those cold menacing crags that kept rushing at us out of the vapor.[3]

Alaskans All was not academic and did not work as a reference. Dates and times were nearly nonexistent. The text and photographs, however, focused on details and anecdotes that, except for Willoughby, might have been lost to Alaskan history. It was the recording of those people and events during that period that was significant. In those nonfiction offerings, Willoughby chronicled first-time events and wrote of courage and kindness.

For example, Willoughby recorded the first air mail flight in Alaska, flown by Ben Eielson who—from above—raced a dog sled mail team on the ground.

> "And," Ben said, flying high above, "I remember when I reached the half way point on the 300-mile route, Lake Minchumina, I looked out at that 16-mile stretch of frozen water, and saw the tiny figures of the regular dog team mail just beginning to cross it going toward McGrath, as I was."
>
> Dog team mail versus airplane mail! The difference in speed may be gauged from the

A pioneer in Alaskan aviation, Carl Ben Eielson was featured in *Alaskans All*. Having met and flown with Eielson, Willoughby later collaborated with Edna Walker Chandler on a juvenile biography about the bush pilot. *Historical Photograph Collection, Rasmuson Library, University of Alaska Fairbanks*

fact that Ben flew against half a gale, delivered his mail at McGrath, attended to some commissions, took a brief part in the celebrations . . . and on his return trip was soaring over Lake Minchumina again before the dog team had finished crossing it![4]

Though her accounts of these unique Alaskans centered on their efforts toward serious endeavors, Willoughby occasionally touched on a lighter side.

Stroller White, for instance, told of his "ice-worm cocktail" at Dawson's Monte Carlo Saloon after he had invented the glacier "ice worm." The bartender handed him his drink and White related:

He handed me my glass. Bracing myself for the ordeal, I gulped the contents, worm and all. It slipped down with horrible ease. The bartender leaned apologetically toward me. "Say, Stroller," he whispered out of the corner of his mouth, "we couldn't get any of the real thing so we faked 'em by poking spaghetti through gimlet holes in the ice, and letting it swell. But for Pete's sake, don't tell any of the boys the difference!"[5]

The nonfiction books were packed with fascinating episodes of Alaskan men and women who—because of their personalities or their deeds—stamped Alaska history with its own unique imprint.

In a April 30, 1933, review of *Alaskans All* by *Book Review Digest*:

When Barrett Willoughby is describing the beauties and scenic marvels of her beloved Alaska, and painting verbally portraits of the gentlemen unafraid, whose initiative and daring have woven into that country's history its most colorful threads, she is at her literary best. . . .[6]

Willoughby's next work, *River House*, changed genre back to the romantic novel. It appeared in serial form in *The Call Bulletin* newspaper under the title "The Captive Bride."[7] The copyright page of *River House* also stated that "Captive Bride" had run in *The American Magazine,* but publication dates were not given.[8]

The dedication of *River House* honored a special poet friend of Willoughby's—"Pat (One-Shot) O'Cotter, Philosopher, Poet, and True Sportsman, With Gratitude for Showing Me the Way to the Stikine." O'Cotter, whose real name was Frank J. Cotter,[9] was a writer himself. He published a poetry book entitled *Rhymes of a Roughneck* (1918). He also wrote a column. "Through Northern Glasses," for the Seattle *Alaska Weekly* during the 1920s.[10]

Action for *River House* took place up the Stikine River outside Wrangell. Willoughby described the waterway as:

> [T]he river itself is a mystic river that seems to have a strange influence on the lives of men. The old timers call it "she." They say, "She's a witch river, and she flows through the sunny land of Don't Give a Damn." That is because so many men go up river for a visit and then stay forever, quite forgetting their homes and families left in the States.[11]

The novel dealt with big-game hunting at a lodge on the Canada-Alaska border. The book jacket capsuled the tale: "Denise Keith came to Alaska prepared to dislike it, but a daring man, and the ever-changing river, and one reckless night of love changed her heart and her mind."[12]

Most of Willoughby's novels occurred over a brief period, often during one season. *River House* was an exception, taking place from August until perhaps May with an emphasis on the fall season. A few narrative sections ground through the story as if they were having difficulty getting through the winter. Also, *River House* came as close to sex as Willoughby ever allowed in her books; it was not the heroine who stopped the advances but the idealized hero.

River House, proved another instant success. Published by Little, Brown in 1936, it was reprinted three times in April, the month it appeared. Soon after, Hutchison of London, England, put out its copy.[13]

Although *The New York Times* thought Willoughby guilty of "overwriting,"[14] all reviewers praised her descriptive passages. *The Boston Transcript's* account was typical:

> The human characters are very real and vital, but the river and the mountains and the forest of Alaska are made even more so. All together, they make a novel as filled with contrasts and many swift alternations of moods and scenes, as the River Stikine itself.[15]

Barrett Willoughby said little in print about book reviews or reviewers. However, she was neither defensive nor cowed by them. They were, to her, part of the profession. Overall, reviewers proved positive—but not all the time. "Some criticized and gave suggestions," reported Willoughby in a newspaper article. She continued,

> One or two poked fun at me, but it was in a rib-nudging, man-to-man way, you understand. The way and the nudging made me grin and squirm at the same time. If there had been too much of it, though, I would have just

Dust jacket cover of *River House*, 1936. *Alaska State Historical Library, Juneau. Photograph by Ed Ferrell*

squirmed—for I'm like everyone else: I'd rather be thought unvirtuous than ridiculous. Some of them said I was melodramatic—and I am. Every Alaskan is melodramatic. We'd rather be that way than static.[16]

She ended the article with a poem which summed up her feelings about her work and book reviews.

This man done his damndest.
Angels can do no more.[17]

It could easily have been this Wrangell research trip (or an earlier one), when Florence met boat operator Earl Bright (who later lived, wrote, and was married under the preferred name of Captain Larry O'Connor).[18] When Willoughby returned to San Francisco, O'Connor was not far behind. He became a kind of secretary to Florence, smoothing travel plans to Mexico, making life a little easier for her. She helped him write a book and encouraged him as an author. He wanted to marry her, but she resisted. In the end, he won.[19] Florence Prosser, then approaching fifty, and Larry O'Connor were married by District Judge B. F. Curler on July 17, 1935, in Reno, Nevada.[20] The two made their home in San Carlos, California.

Florence was attracted to this "world wandering adventurer"[21] and compared him to her father. In a 1939 radio interview she said of her relationship with Larry:

Though we do not collaborate on stories we derive much fun and profit from criticizing each other's manuscripts and acting out the scenes in our stories. I use my married name only when traveling. Each time either of us finishes a long story, we cast responsibility to the winds and go roaming sometimes in our car, sometimes on a cruiser. We never make any plans for these jaunts—the gods of chance decide our itinerary.[22]

Willoughby's real-life California living might best be imagined as heroine Lynn described it in *The Golden Totem*:

[H]er heart kept turning back to the pleasant life they had known together in [Aunt] Julie's small balconied house on the slope of a Berkeley hill; sunny rooms lined with books, filled with flowers and sprinkled with pages of manuscript that were forever escaping from Julie's study. . . . Minor celebrations that marked the completion of each story: people flocking in, music and gaiety and everybody munching sandwiches and trailing Julie about so they wouldn't miss any of the amusing things she said. Major celebrations following the receipt of a story check: new clothes, books, perfumes, and the two of them going off to Yosemite, to Lake Tahoe, to Palm Springs, staying always at the luxury hotels and living the life of Riley as long as the money lasted. It never occurred to Julie to save a dollar . . . [23]

Florence's actual San Carlos home itself was tucked on a rather wild bench overlooking a lovely valley in the San Francisco Bay area. It was a spacious split-level with an apartment below. The house screened the driveway which curved around the front, affording privacy. Large windows let in light, and comfortable, expensive furniture invited lounging.[24]

Barrett Willoughby's strong-willed mother managed the housekeeping. She often disapproved of her daughter's open and generous attitude toward people employed around the home. "Barrie spoiled every maid I ever hired," she complained.[25] It seemed Barrett Willoughby considered people as friends rather than servants and bent over backwards to help them whenever possible.

In the midst of her happy marriage and successful writing career, Willoughby was saddened by the death of her stepfather of heart failure on January 13, 1938. A celebrity in his own right, Charles Willoughby was remembered as a daring sea captain, head of the first life saving station at Cape Flattery, Washington, and Klondike adventurer.[26]

Explorer though Charles might have been, businessman he was not. When he originally moved to California, he pushed to start a silver fox ranch. Barrett Willoughby staked him. The business did not flourish and soon went broke. This venture further depleted Willoughby's financial resources.[27]

The Willoughby/O'Connor household went on in its routine. The year following Charles's death, Little, Brown published *Sondra O'Moore*, a novel of spies, smuggling and romance in the Sitka, Alaska, area. The book price at that time was $2.00.[28] When the novel appeared, *The Alaska Weekly* proclaimed: "Once Again Alaska's Favorite Writer Hits the Bull's-Eye With a Stirring Tale of Old and Modern Sitka, Just Off the Press."[29] In true romantic style, the book ended with the heroine and hero alone on the deck of the boat *Glory*: "And then, in the moonlight, the two laid but a single, still shadow on the *Glory's* deck."[30]

Sondra O'Moore was serialized in *The American Magazine* under the title, "Lover Come Back,"[31] and was dedicated to "Larry O'Connor—with laughter."

Willoughby admitted that the character "Sondra" was patterned after her red-headed niece and namesake, who

The Governor's House at Sitka. This mansion could have been the model for Echo House, the base of operations in Willoughby's novel, *Sondra O'Moore*. *Barrett Willoughby Photograph Collection, Rasmuson Library, University of Alaska Fairbanks*

was brother Lawrence's daughter.[32] Niece Florence, who went by the name of "Beau," was cared for by Barrett Willoughby for a while after Lawrence died.[33]

Beau loved and spoke nothing but praise for her aunt: "[H]er friends adored her and she never missed an opportunity to show her love for family and friends."[34] About Willoughby's writing she said, "She caught the real pioneer spirit in the characters she created and she enjoyed her work. It was her life. She loved Alaska."[35]

In 1940, Little, Brown published Willoughby's *Alaska Holiday*. Again, sections of the book appeared in magazines either before or after publication. *Readers' Digest*, for example, reprinted "One Alaska Night"—a story about a girl lost in the wilderness who comes upon the cabin of a crazy trapper—three years after the book's appearance (February 1943).[36] *The American Magazine,* on the other hand, printed "I'm a Cream-puff Pioneer"—a story about a lady farmer living in the Matanuska Valley— three years before (June 1937).[37]

The Alaska Weekly, ever a Willoughby supporter, said, "[The book] starts, as do most of Willoughby's stories, like a snowslide breaking loose in Moose Pass, and carries on to the last page with a like speed."[38]

While Willoughby's other nonfiction books focused primarily on biographical material, *Alaska Holiday* contained more variety. It included Willoughby's autobiographical adventures and Alaskan subjects such as totem poles and seal colonies of the Pribilof Islands. In addition, she included biographical information on lighthouse keeper Ted Pedersen, farmer Mrs. Victor Johnson, and dance-hall entertainer Klondike Kate. Twenty-five black and white photographs enhanced the material.

As in previous nonfiction writings, Willoughby followed the same success formula—few sources but absorbing experiences. Take, for instance, one from earlier days when lighthouses were actually manned. Unimak lighthouse keeper Ted Pedersen described a black September's night when his lighthouse was deluged by birds, thrown off their migration course and drawn to the beacon light.

> I was looking out the window to see if our beam was piercing the darkness as it should, when I noticed a queer flickering of the light ray. I stepped outside to investigate, and found the air literally alive with thousands of tiny birds, evidently off their course on their migration south. The next instant I was standing in the midst of a deluge of birds that dashed blindly against our plate-glass light cage and the lighted lower windows of the watch room. . . . [39]

Klondike Kate, who danced in Dawson saloons during the stampeding days, was one of the colorful characters included in Willoughby's book, *Alaska Holiday*. Kate said, "We wore tights in those days. If we hadn't the Mounted Police would have run us out of the country." *Barrett Willoughby Photograph Collection, Rasmuson Library, University of Alaska Fairbanks*

Through her writings, Willoughby preserved and presented part of Alaskan history for future readers. Some of her topics may have been covered in more depth through scientific journals or academia but not in such a readable fashion for the general public.

Alaska Holiday was reprinted several times. *The New Yorker* (May 1940) said:

> Miss Willoughby writes with zip and charm and while this is not a travel book in the staid sense of the word, it does take the reader traveling to strange and interesting and little-known places.[40]

Ted Pedersen became a friend of Barrett Willoughby's. When *Alaska Holiday* came out, she sent him a book with the following inscription:

> For Ted who has lived more exciting adventures than I have ever written. Remember, you Alaskan, you are the captain and it's up to you to keep to your course. Bon Voyage, Barrie.[41]

During one visit to the San Francisco area, Ted met Elsa Kienitz through a mutual friend, and they were married at Willoughby's San Carlos home in 1942.[42]

An even longer-lasting friendship developed between Florence and Elsa Pedersen who herself had a desire to write. Willoughby was delighted and encouraged Elsa with advice and suggestions.[43] Elsa became a well-known Alaskan author in her own right with a string of juvenile novels to her credit. *Dangerous Flight*, her second book, was dedicated to the memory of Barrett Willoughby.[44]

9

A Disenchanted Lady

A war raged in Europe during the same period that Willoughby fans read of sourdoughs and dance hall girls. Few American readers, and certainly British ones, were untouched in some way by World War II. Perhaps Willoughby's books afforded a romantic escape from the pressing realities of everyday life.

Barrett Willoughby was a successful writer, but it was not her fate to sail a smooth matrimonial sea. Larry, it appeared, was doing his own skylarking with the ladies, buying roses on the sly, and unknown to Willoughby, having her pay the bills.[1] After their marriage, Florence had bought Larry a furniture store, and he eventually ran off with the bookkeeper.[2] The O'Connors were divorced in 1942.[3]

Florence said for several years she knew matters were wrong between them. Besides the emotional distancing, she watched her money disappear. O'Connor the charmer, the promoter, had little sense when it came to high finance. He manipulated bonds Florence had set aside for her senior years, speculated, and lost everything.[4] He urged Florence to sell properties and stocks until she had little left. She spoke of obtaining a loan on her life insurance, of selling the house and of moving south with her mother,[5] who was about seventy-five years old at the time.

When divorce legalities were settled, Florence marshalled her spirits and brought herself up from these matrimonial and financial setbacks. She wrote to niece Beau:

> I'm working like hell and am more alive and alert than I've been for seven years! And I'm captain of the *Barrett Willoughby* again, a funny little cruiser that's been floundering about for a long time, with no steady hand at the wheel. And by hell, the first one I find pitying me, I'm going to punch them in the nose![6]

It was like Willoughby, in spite of Larry's betrayal, to forgive him or at least excuse some of his actions. Further in the letter to Beau she wrote:

> I feel no resentment against Larry, I was just dumb. He was always kind to you kids. He is a fine companion, a good story teller. He gave me great happiness for awhile—but I imagine he got tired—and then there were too many poor widows, etc., depending on him for comfort and advice—so he had to neglect something. And so—we write finis to that.[7]

There was little doubt that Willoughby was drawn to adventuring men—those of a carefree, irresponsible nature. They were gamblers at heart (like her father) and did not lean heavily to the practicalities of life.

Florence might have realized this need in her and was honest enough to excuse those traits in her husbands. It was part of their charm.

A thoughtful Willoughby poses in front of a mission—probably Carmel, California, before 1937. *Courtesy of Helen Smith Scudder*

It was also like Willoughby, once down, to gather her forces and work up a positive attitude. She wrote Beau:

> But I feel grand, really. My old bean is click-
> ing again the way it used to. And something
> calls from over the top of the hill again—some-
> thing lovely and clean and gay and romantic. I
> don't know what it is exactly—but some fine
> venture.[8]

Willoughby tried to maintain a positive view and was successful much of the time. On rare occasions disappoint-ment showed through. The dedication in her last full adult book, *The Golden Totem*, spoke to this melancholy: "To a cheerful, disenchanted lady—myself."

Willoughby was counting on *The Golden Totem* to help recoup finances after her divorce.[9] Records showed that only one article bearing her byline appeared in the five-year period between her last books—1940 to 1945.

Luckily her new novel was another success, being re-printed four times within several months of publication. But then, Willoughby always said she was lucky. In a 1925 interview, and in subsequent talks, she said:

> The most marvelous luck has attended me
> in my short writing career. Perhaps its because
> I'm always expecting it. I'm the kind of person
> who, if she'd fall in the ocean, would bob up
> with a string of pearls about her neck.[10]

The Golden Totem, set in Juneau, Alaska, was brought out by Little, Brown in 1945. A serial version of the novel was syndicated by *The Chicago Tribune*.[11]

The book dealt with the romance and adventure gen-erated by gold mining activities. As the story unfolded, the Golden Totem Mine was being taken over through

Dust jacket of The Golden Totem, 1945. Alaska State Historical
Library, Juneau. Photograph by Ed Ferrell

illicit means, and the heroine, in spite of several love conflicts, helped save the day. It was formula Willoughby, for
the most part, but exciting and absorbing nevertheless.

In previous novels, the reader might easily imagine
Willoughby placing herself in the role of the romantic,
fictionalized heroine, and she did this through Lynn in
The Golden Totem, too. But there was a flashback scene at
the onset that showed Willoughby's disenchanted attitude
through the cynical, fictional author, Aunt Julie, living
in California. Heroine Lynn had remembered her aunt
saying:

> "Love? Marriage?" She would flash
> matchmakers the rueful and derisive little grin
> that always accompanied her thought of the
> charming drunkard and gentleman bum who,
> briefly, had been her husband. "What is there
> to marriage but the honeymoon? A flight by
> moonlight. Then—daybreak; heartbreak. No,
> boys and girls. No more of that for me. I'm
> satisfied with my writing and my Lynn."[12]

Here again, Willoughby's scenic descriptions stand out.
As the *Weekly Book Review* (March 18, 1945) stated: "[T]he
real heroine of *The Golden Totem* is Alaska herself."[13] And
The New York Times (March 11, 1945) agreed:

> There is something in the Willoughby books
> reminiscent of the old C. N. and A. M.
> Williamson days when scenery played the lead-
> ing role and love-making was achieved between
> vivid landscapes.[14]

A month after *The Golden Totem* came out, Willoughby
already planned on writing a novel located in Sitka, Alaska.
To that end, she gathered materials and studied at the
California State Library in Sacramento.[15]

ALASKA SEAS

Starring

ROBERT RYAN
JAN STERLING
BRIAN KEITH
GENE BARRY

Produced by Mel Epstein
Directed by Jerry Hopper
Screenplay by Geoffrey Homes
and Walter Doniger
Based on a story by Barrett Willoughby
A PARAMOUNT PICTURE

Because Barrett Willoughby sold all movie rights to *Spawn of the North,* she did not gain financially when the remake, under the title, *Alaska Seas,* came out in 1954. This is a poster publicizing the film. *Paramount Pictures, Inc. Photograph by Ed Ferrell*

Barrett Willoughby's mother, Florence senior, died some time in the next ten years. California vital records do not reveal where or when. The only reference to the death was in a letter Barrett wrote from La Canada, California, in October of 1956. In the letter she stated, "Besides, I feel closer to mamma up there [San Francisco] where there are no sad memories of her long, last sickness."[16] Barrett Willoughby was nearing sixty.

Barrett Willoughby produced no more best-selling books for the remaining fifteen years of her life. There was an occasional piece such as "The Snow Woman and Mary Hewitt," published in the December 1953 issue of *The Alaska Sportsman* magazine.[17]

Barrett Willoughby collaborated with Edna Walker Chandler on
Willoughby's last book, *Pioneer of Alaska Skies*. Published by Ginn
and Company, the book came out in 1959, shortly after
Willoughby's death. *Juneau (Alaska) Public Library. Photograph by
Ed Ferrell*

The early 1950s saw a remake of Paramount's and Willoughby's *Spawn of the North* movie, under the name of *Alaska Seas*. Stars were listed as Robert Ryan, Brian Keith, and Jan Sterling.[18] Florence received no money from this film.

When Willoughby called herself "the disenchanted lady," it was not entirely because of disappointments with love. While she had worked hard for the high points in life, circumstances and a few bad decisions had given her the downside, too. She had spent a good share of her adult life taking care of other people financially; what savings she had amassed had been squandered by her fourth husband.

A further disenchantment was the fact that the times had changed; Willoughby's style of writing was no longer in vogue. There was evidence that she continued her personal writing—working sheets of summaries, drafts, revisions among the papers she left behind—but no sales. The last decade of her life was leaner than she had planned.

To earn a living, Elsa Pedersen said Florence worked for others in the Los Angeles area during that time. She researched, prepared movie scripts, and subcontracted to a more successful writer[19]—possibly Adela Rogers St. John, who was a good friend. Willoughby never stopped writing, but she produced no more books.

Elsa Pedersen gave insight into Willoughby's situation:

> Barrie lost contact with Alaska at the start of World War II, and had difficulty realizing how much the country had changed. . . . The reason little is known about the last ten years of [her] life is that she wanted it that way. She worked hard to be a successful writer and was well aware that current affairs made her talents obsolete.[20]

In spite of harder times, Willoughby never lost her enthusiasm nor the anticipation that something good was around the next corner. When a positive event occurred, Florence was all excitement.

In 1956 Willoughby—then close to seventy years old— said she was back on the writing track once more:

> I'm a writer again! I finished a piece and my agent sold it to *Good Housekeeping*—who will cut it and let me approve the cutting—and I got three times more for it almost then for the last piece I finished and sold them years ago. Callo! Calley! One never knows until they prove it that one has not lost the touch after a period of non-writing![21]

Moments of success fired her for other projects. On one, she worked in collaboration with Edna W. Chandler on a juvenile book featuring pilot Carl Ben Eielson.

Plans did not stop with the Eielson book. Although Jack London died (1916) before Willoughby located to California, some time later she moved in London's social circle. Florence developed a friendship with London's wife, Charmian, and his nephew Irving Shepard (Shep). Although Charmian was a writer herself, Barrett Willoughby proposed doing a biography about her[22] and later suggested a juvenile book on Jack London. All these plans were submitted to Shep who had control of Charmian's diaries.

Willoughby was sorry she had not spent more time at the London ranch with Charmian in earlier years but had good reason:

> I've been reading over Charmian's letters to me. And seeing how warm she was always inviting me up to the Ranch. How I wish I could have gone more often. But I had so many people to support, I had to stick right to the Corona.

BARRETT WILLOUGHBY, a native Alaskan, brings to this book not only a rich background and love of Alaska, but a personal friendship with its subject, Ben Eielson. She has written many books and articles about Alaska and Alaskans.

Photograph and information about Barrett Willoughby appeared on the book flap of *Pioneer of Alaska Skies. Juneau (Alaska) Public Library. Photograph by Ed Ferrell*

And then my folks were always being sick, too. And I was never easy away from them.[23]

Ever the worker, Willoughby spent weeks reading background material on London and outlining an approach to the forthcoming books.

In July of 1956, *Good Housekeeping Magazine* printed Willoughby's final article, which she titled, "Papa and the Reluctant Pioneer," and which the publisher changed to "Papa Came C.O.D."[24] The piece highlighted the Martin Barrett family during the early days of adventuring in Alaska and gave insights into the parents' relationship.

Most of Willoughby's last writings were completed in the Los Angeles area (La Canada). Florence could hardly wait until she moved back north to San Francisco again.

> I'm just dying to get away from this southern country and up to the Bay region. Some days I can hardly stand it down here another minute. I feel as though I were stuffed with cold boiled potatoes and my brain was a piece of Swiss cheese—In other words, static. However, I'll soon get my business cleared up down here. And then—me for San Francisco!![25]

At some point in the Shep/Willoughby plans and negotiations for the two books, Shep mentioned going fifty/fifty on the financial arrangements. Willoughby's answer was telling to the practical side of her nature:

> [W]hen you were here, Shep, you mentioned something about going fifty-fifty on the book. I assumed that meant on the proceeds, not on the expenses incurred in writing the book.[26]

Willoughby then explained to him that:

> Taxes, insurance and maintenance leave me very little to live on. And I'm always worried about paying my rent, and about housecleaning costs. And about eating—because I can't cook and must be near a restaurant.[27]

A few lines later in the letter, Willoughby then told Shep what financial arrangements were necessary in order for her to write the books. The plans called for him to "grubstake" her by paying certain expenses every month, and then she would be willing to go fifty/fifty on the book.[28] Perhaps Shep was agreeable, for negotiations and friendship continued. Negotiations proved easier than composition, for she never completed a book on Jack or Charmian London.

Finally, by January 1957, Florence was moved to a tower view apartment in her "beloved San Francisco."[29] At the time she was trying to sell her San Carlos home, as " . . . it's too much for me to keep up now that I'm alone."[30] Willoughby might have been living alone, but she spoke of cousins in the California area so there were relatives nearby.[31]

Barrett Willoughby lived two more years before her heart gave out at the age of seventy-three. When she died at 2:30 A.M. on July 29, 1959, it was at the Alta Bates Hospital, Berkeley. Her death certificate noted the vanity errors she carried in life—a 1900 birth date, an Alaska birthplace, and an English mother. The O'Connor marriage was omitted entirely, for she was listed as Mrs. Robert Prosser.[32] Niece Beau said that even at her death, Florence was taking a writing course.[33]

As a kind of last testimonial to her writing career, the Ben Eielson book came out soon after her death.[34] It, like her other works, was Alaskan to the core.

Though Willoughby lost touch with Alaska during her later years, she never forgot it. Bob Henning, former editor/publisher of *The Alaska Sportsman* magazine recalled correspondence with Willoughby several months before she died.

In 1959, Henning restyled the title on the magazine cover, highlighting a red "*A*" at the beginning of the word

"Alaska," and coloring the other letters blue. Willoughby wrote Henning from California saying she played a game with herself; when she walked past a newsstand she would see how fast she could spot the red and blue title. She further said the red letter reminded her of the Alaskan sunset, the blue letters its northern sky.[35]

An underlying vein of nostalgia wove through Willoughby's life and through her books. She tried to hold onto the excitement of those earlier days, relive the past through her youthful heroines.

But the world had changed by the mid-twentieth century.

Many misty idealized concepts held by the public gave way under the stark focus of realities during the Great Depression and World War II. Advanced transportation and travel, too, brought foreign lands closer; the far away was not quite so far away, the unique not quite so untouchable. The rosy glow of romance had withered at the edges.

Willoughby's time had come and gone.

ALASKA BOOKS

By BARRETT WILLOUGHBY

Sondra O'Moore

This is a story of a grand girl and a grand old man —a thrilling land-and-sea story of Alaskan fisheries. The exciting episodes of a feud between two rival fishing fleets, with the truly dramatic chase at sea, could only be described by a person who knows Alaska and its people. 320 pages........ $2.00

River House

A stirring novel with the Stikine River for its setting. Seldom has environment moulded character as does the Stikine in this story. The River is almost the leading character, but whether as hero or villain, it is hard to judge. By one of the best informed writers on Alaska today. 389 pages.....85c

Spawn of the North

This book gives intimate glimpses into the salmon industry of Ketchikan. An enthralling romance and dramatic action are interwoven. Made into a motion picture by Paramount, a tale of wild excitement which is climaxed with the salmon run and feud between two strong men. 349 pages.........85c

Alaska Holiday

A chronicle of bright Alaska days that reads like a novel, with chapters depicting a lighthouse amid active volcanoes, mating time of the great seal herd, totem-pole superstitions, and incomparable Klondike Kate, dance hall girl of the Gold-rush. You'll like this zestful, colorful book. 296 pages. Illustrated $3.00

Sitka, Portal to Romance

In this book runs the charm of serene Alaska of the Russian days. Here are stories of old Sitka obtained from descendants of the men who ruled in days of Sea otter hunting, traders, and gentleman adventurers. A factual story by Alaska's most popular author. Illustrated. 233 pages...............$3.50

THE ALASKA SPORTSMAN
Box 118, Ketchikan, Alaska

Advertisement in *The Alaska Sportsman,* January 1946. *Alaska Collection, Rasmuson Library, University of Alaska Fairbanks*

10

Inside Willoughby's Books

Barrett Willoughby was, above everything else, a romantic writer. She emphasized the exciting exploits of outstanding Alaskans, and she crafted adventures for her set of fiction characters. While her descriptions of northern life (fox farming, gold mining, commercial fishing, dog sled racing, big game hunting) proved realistic, they were used to serve her romantic writing. These activities were out of the commonplace and from a non-Alaskan view, mysterious and exotic.

Writing articles, taking writing courses at college, and working for Frederick O'Brien helped to prepare Barrett Willoughby as a fiction and nonfiction author. Although her writing style did not change drastically over her career, she never stopped crafting her art. Her vocabulary delivered the correct nuance; her story progressed logically; her dialogue rang true. As her career advanced, a slightly more sophisticated tone polished her words as it polished her life.

Barrett Willoughby first gained her national reputation as a nonfiction writer, penning Alaskan articles for magazines. A number of her nonfiction pieces were later compiled into books. For example, "Scotty" Allan was the subject of an article which

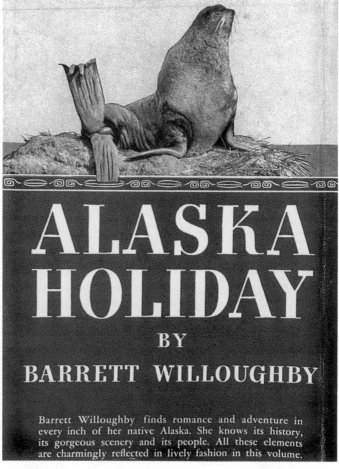

Dust jacket of *Alaska Holiday,* 1940. *Courtesy of Joan Buhler. Photograph by Paul Boyer*

appeared in the February 1921 issue of *Sunset Magazine*; the dog sled racer later appeared in a section of Willoughby's book, *Gentlemen Unafraid,* published in 1928.

The very choice of Willoughby's nonfiction subjects further defined her as a romantic author. The topics of her pieces were men, women, and places larger than life—

certainly light years from the everyday existence experienced by most Americans. These subjects were the epitome of what Willoughby thought symbolized Alaska—romance, adventure, and extremes.

Other people, too, saw the awe in Willoughby's work. An *Alaska Weekly* reporter reviewing *Gentlemen Unafraid* wrote:

> Her father, so well known to former residents of Katalla and Cordova, is given a deserved tribute from an adoring daughter, and George Watkins Evans is surrounded by a halo of girlish worship.[1]

Although a few dates and place names punctuate the author's nonfiction pieces, the articles were not meant for reference study. Willoughby filled the narrative with description and information. The style was conversational rather than academic. The glacier priest, Father Bernard Hubbard, for instance, related his astounded impression of the Katmai area after its volcanic explosion in 1912.

> I've talked with men who hunted in this valley before the eruption when it lay green and beautiful between spruce-ranked mountains.
>
> But the next morning, when we looked out of our cave, this is what we saw: Blue sky, pearl-toned clouds, and the sun pouring down into the Valley of Ten Thousands Smokes. It spread before us, seven miles wide, seventeen miles long, and not a sprig of vegetation visible in all its strange sweep. On either side rose a line of lofty, smoking mountains, with ash-yellow slopes hung with snow fields and crystal glaciers. The feet of those volcanoes were gashed

Authority on volcanoes and glaciers, lecturer, and Jesuit priest, Father Bernard R. Hubbard and his exploits appeared in Willoughby's *Alaskans All. Barrett Willoughby Photograph Collection, Rasmuson Library, University of Alaska Fairbanks*

with fissures red as blood. The smooth valley floor was yellow, but punctured with fumaroles ringed with red, blue, violet and orange—hundreds of vents sending up billows of steam.[2]

Willoughby researched her subjects both on scene and in libraries, concentrating to find the right word, to craft the imaginative phrase. She also snapped many of the black and white photographs enhancing her work, including those taken on a trip to Siberia. What material she gathered on these trips frequently became background for her fiction books. For example, material in *Sitka, Portal to Romance* was used as a basis for the novel, *Sondra O'Moore*. Information from Syd Barrington and a trip up the Stikine River gave setting to her story, *River House*.

The activities of many of the unusual Alaskans Willoughby wrote about might have been lost entirely, except for her having recorded them when she did. Certainly anecdotal information—told by the subjects themselves—never would have survived.

However, Barrett Willoughby earned her greatest following through her novels. From the beginning of her fiction career, Willoughby found a story line pattern which brought her wide readership and, essentially, she stuck with it. There were few striking variations.

Though roughly, with her first novel—*Where the Sun Swings North*—and then with more confidence in *Rocking Moon*, Willoughby worked this story line and its cast of characters in all her fiction. Generally Willoughby kept the story line the same and set her characters in new locations. For instance, her cast of characters traveled to Sitka for *Sondra O'Moore*, to Juneau for *The Golden Totem*, to Middleton Island for *Where the Sun Swings North*. The descriptions and activities of the diverse locations added the variety and uniqueness to her works. Barrett Willoughby explains,

> In a land one-fifth as large as the whole United States, with winters varying from those as mild as Northern California to those as severe as Kamchatka, it stands to reason that each locality leaves its own particular stamp upon the inhabitants. A story of Southeastern Alaska

Willoughby stands before the heavy door of the old Russian saltry in Sitka in the late 1920s. The door is discussed in *Sitka, Portal to Romance*. At the time, the building was a private home. *Courtesy of Dee Longenbaugh*

would be no more like a story of the Aleutian
Islands than one of Texas would be like the
story of Massachusetts.[3]

And Willoughby handled those Alaskan elements—
description and activity—with professional excellence.

A major contrast in all of Willoughby's fiction books
dealt with place. Alaska, the wild land of adventure, freedom and survival, contrasted with the settled, practical,
safe life in California.

Willoughby lived in both places, and she brought this
contrast to her books. Most of her heroines and some of
her characters had an attachment to California in one way
or another. In the end a central character had a decision
to make—Would it be Alaska or California?

In *River House*, for instance, Willoughby compared dif-
fering views of the Stikine River to contrast Alaska with
California. Heroine Denny's divorced mother, while re-
laxing on a chaise lounge receiving a beauty treatment in
California, confided to her daughter:

> The Stikine—it's a witch river. Dangerous.
> Cruel. Whispering over dead men's bones. It
> puts a spell on you, Denny. . . . It won your
> father from me.[4]

And her Alaskan father's view of the same waterway:

> I'll take you home to the river some day—a
> river that rises in a man's dreams and flows
> straight through his heart. Jade-white she is;
> born of glacier and wid [sic] silver poplars
> laughin' on her banks. There's never a stream
> in all the world as beautiful and beguiling.[5]

After thinking over these two conversations, Denny
asked herself: "Which river am I going to find?"[6]

In *The Golden Totem*, the southern boyfriend, Perry, stated the Alaska/California contrast more pointedly in a proposal to heroine Lynn:

> "Here's what I mean, Lynn: two roads are opening up before you at this moment. One," he held up a forefinger—"you can stick here in California surrounded by climate, civilization, commonplaces. Two," he held up the other forefinger—"you can marry me and we'll shove off for Alaska together to seek our fortune."[7]

The story line formula with its cast of characters was generally based on: a young idealized heroine who had attachments to California; two rival men she must choose between; a bad girl contrast to the heroine; a present or absent Irish father/relative; a rough diamond housekeeper/cook with or without a husband; a love or fiance in California.

Willoughby's heroines were idealized. Physically, there were some variations such as hair color or face shape. But they all had little hands, fingers, ears, and feet, and were small and slim in stature. Not beautiful, they possessed attributes which caught a man's eye and made him look twice. Character Jefferson Greer best expressed this idealization when speaking with heroine Lynn in *The Golden Totem*:

> "Because at last I have found my ideal woman," he said in his quiet, rich-fibered voice. "Oh, I know that sounds sentimental and old-fashioned to you, Lynn. But every man has his ideal woman; the one he longs for, searches for, even in his teens. . . .To us, our ideal becomes the end and aim of existence. Some of us never find her. But I found her. I looked up one day—and there she was."

He gave a low, bemused laugh. "She's little, and gay, and her short hair is so fine that when she runs bareheaded it slides about all silky and bright and confused. You'd think, to look at her, that she's helpless, a satin-and-velvet little lady. But that's only on the outside. She's independent, and fiercely proud, and I'd stake everything I own on her being a square shooter. A trait rare in women."[8]

In addition, the heroines were optimistic—like Willoughby herself—and always expectant about something to happen:

Every hour she felt as if she were on the brink of something wonderful, quite unprecedented *(Spawn of the North)*.[9]

Again she had that magical sense of coming close to some wonderful secret that lay for her divining under the physical aspect of this country *(River House)*.[10]

She felt again that wondering anticipation of the unknown which the advent of Miss Jacqueline never failed to arouse in her. Something was going to happen *(Sondra O'Moore)*.[11]

Men loved and protected Willoughby's heroines. Yet, in spite of a certain dependency in the women, they could call up a stiff backbone when needed. Barbee, in *The Trail Eater*, bolstered her courage after being humiliated:

Was she going to allow herself to be broken under the first blow Fate had dealt her?

Dust jacket of *Sondra O'Moore*, 1939. *Alaska State Historical Library, Juneau. Photograph by Ed Ferrell*

She straightened her shoulders. Pride stirred
in her again. She must not allow Kerry or anyone else to know how she had been hurt, humiliated, disillusioned today.[12]

A step further demonstrated the self-reliance in
Willoughby's heroines. Could author Willoughby be ex-
pressing her own independence when she wrote of Gary
thinking about Sasha in *Rocking Moon*:

> Sasha always insisted on helping everyone, man
> or woman, and in return she expected their
> co-operation in whatever she happened to be
> doing. To the little Alaskan there was no such
> thing as "woman's" work and "man's" work. It
> was all "our" work.[13]

Men, too, were idealized by Willoughby's heroines.
Judge this thought expressed by Sondra in *Sondra O'Moore*:

> This was the hour that had always brought
> romance near to her—that lover she had fash-
> ioned from dreams: Daring, wise, gentle, strong.
> Capable of commanding dangerous men, yet
> yielding to one woman—herself. Even when
> her reason had flouted his existence, her heart
> had believed he was out there somewhere; and
> one day he would come to claim her.[14]

While male villains were not idealized, they had a certain sensitivity, and they were never totally cruel. Consider villain Jim as he spoke with a cohort in *Rocking Moon*:

> "You should worry about any more all night
> business, Mack. This is the last haul of the sea-
> son—and now we can loaf while the Boss runs

the risk," declared Jim. "Speakin' of sleep—I wonder how that poor boob of a cheechako is restin' now. Gosh, I hated to bean that guy, someway, him sittin' there so chummy with that little runt fox. . . . Kinda wish I'd put his coat over him—it's gettin' colder 'n blazes out."[15]

An overview of Willoughby's central characters would not be complete without a brief note of the bad girl in her novels. Willoughby colored these females with vivid traits as a foil to her ideal heroines. One could wonder whether the "other woman" might not be Willoughby's own alter ego.

Principally, these "bad" females drank too much, were divorcees, were by far too flamboyant, had seen their best years, were takers instead of givers, and lacked morals. In short, they were more egocentric than the heroines. They had names like Kitty, Eve, Zoya, Rio, Liane, and Stella. Willoughby, for example, wrote about Stella—as she told an off-color joke to Dr. Baxter in *The Golden Totem*:

> She told it to him as she mounted the stairs beside him, her arm through his, her protu-berant red lips against his ear, murmuring just loud enough so that the others could not fail to catch the biological drift of her humor.
>
> She looked beautiful and opulent in the way a full-blown jacqueminot rose does just before the petals begin to fall.[16]

It was not perhaps Willoughby's characters that showed variety and depth, though some reviewers thought so. Instead, it was Willoughby's fervent background descrip-tions of Alaska and its activities—so unique to the every-day American.

Tyler Kemerlee, for example, told Eve about fish traps on the river in *Spawn of the North*, after fish pirates had struck:

> Well, Eve, for the benefit of a little cheechako like you, I'll explain that fishtraps, as a rule, are always placed in wild, lonely places far from canneries and other habitations; some in hidden inlets, some on the open coast.
>
> It's a standing trap, you know, perhaps three hundred feet offshore—a fish-pound made by driven piles hung with webbing, and covering an area—oh, bigger than a church. Men who watch standing traps don't live right on them as do the watchmen on the floating type.[17]

More exciting were some of Willoughby's descriptions such as ice breaking from the Stikine in *River House*:

> [T]he frozen river began to heave with a leisurely, awesome strength, like that of a Frankenstein quickening into life; gently at first, then with jerks and detonations like cannon fire. Suddenly the entire white surface was broken into segments like a giant jigsaw puzzle, and dark water boiled up between. With the deliberate action of a slowed moving picture, the cakes began to slide downstream—thousands of huge, glittering blocks lazily tilting up on edge; crawling over one another; climbing one another's backs to heights of ten, twenty feet; and crashing down to begin all over again. . . . [18]

For the most part, Willoughby's main characters settled in one building for the story. In *River House*, it was a hunting lodge up the Stikine River; in *Where the Sun Swings North*,

Nome sled dog racer Scotty Allan supplied information and atmosphere for several of Willoughby's fiction and nonfiction pieces. He and his dogs traveled to France during World War I and earned a medal from the French government for their heroic work under fire. *Historical Photograph Collection, Rasmuson Library, University of Alaska Fairbanks*

an abandoned cabin on Middleton Island; in *Rocking Moon* a fox farm on Kodiak Island; in *Spawn of the North* a cannery outside Ketchikan; in *Sondra O'Moore* a mansion on the Sitka waterfront; in *The Golden Totem* a lodge near Juneau. Only one novel—*The Trail Eater*—used a variety of physical locations in and outside Nome.

Despite paragraphs of description, the pace of her stories clipped along at a fair speed. Willoughby studied and applied writing techniques in order to grab readers and hold their interest. As an example, she used cliff hangers at chapter ends to lead the reader into the next section. Judge from this chapter end in *Rocking Moon* as Seenia, an Aleut

woman, tells a group about spirits and the lost Mask of
Jade:

> Everyone in the room was under the old
> Aleut's witch-like spell. Everyone was listen-
> ing, even as she was listening. Again the bell
> outside sounded its single, dim stroke as if a
> spirit hand had touched it. Then Gary stiffened
> as if from an electric shock.
>
> There had been no sound of footsteps on
> the porch, but someone—something—was
> knocking at the door![19]

And again, when heroine Lynn was working a cruiser
through a roaring tide rip in *The Golden Totem*:

> The eddy! Lynn remembered it with won-
> der. We're in the eddy. We're safe!
>
> And then, as she drew a long breath of re-
> lief, the *Stardust* plunged again into the mon-
> strous current that clutched it, twisting it, shook
> it as a terrier shakes a rat, then rose up to climb,
> black and frothing, over the cruiser's bow.
>
> Lynn gripped her hand-hold, braced herself,
> and closed her eyes.
>
> She thought: This is the end.[20]

In exciting spots, Willoughby wrung the scene for every drop of suspense. Her sentences grew shorter, as if
breathless from the pace. She shifted scenes to keep the
reader's interest; in *The Trail Eater*, during the final hours
of the dog sled race, Willoughby shifted scenes five times
in one chapter. The following piece from *The Trail Eater*,
near the end of the book, provides a good example of her
heavy but adept hand at controlling pace. Kerry and his

dog team were overtaking a rival dog team and its driver, Slim:

> Details of Slim's outfit grew clearer—the flapping of his parka skirt, the white square with the numeral "3" on his back. It was plain that he was near the breaking point. He was yelling; looking wildly around; hobbling a few steps behind the sled, then riding the runners despite the labored gait of his dogs. He was unwinding the whip from his waist. He was swinging it across the backs of his malamutes. Shouts. Curses. The tired yip of a whipped dog who is doing his best.
>
> "Tokon, we've got him! When Slim Carvey begins driving with leather we've got him, boy!"
>
> When Kerry hit the lagoon Slim was nearly half way across it. The leaders of both teams knew they were nearing the climax of that gruelling, four hundred mile race. There was a deadly earnestness in their gasping tugs.
>
> The lightness of Kerry's sled was telling. The distance between them shortened.
>
> A hundred feet to go!
>
> Seventy-five!
>
> Fifty feet![21]

Willoughby demonstrated her image of Alaska through her characters, too. Court, in *The Golden Totem*, explained the call of Alaska to heroine Lynn. His dialogue captured the Alaskan image as Outsiders might conceive it at that time in history.

> "When you were in the States you doubtless heard many people say: 'Alaska! Oh, I've always wanted to go there!'" He mimicked

perfectly the slightly heavy, cultured tones of the typical club matron.

"Of course. I've often said it myself."

"There you are—the something which impelled you to speak that way was the Call. Now the Spell is different. That's what Alaska does to you after you get here. I speak for men, of course, since feminine reactions are always mysterious and unpredictable.

"The Spell is made up of a lot of things— freedom from restrictions; building a home from forest trees on land that is free for the taking; living off the country with the only outlay the price of a gun, a fishnet, and a clam shovel. Getting money, when needed, from fishing, or trapping, or panning gold. And breathing air so clean it makes you feel you're on laughing terms with storms, and resilient enough to play leapfrog with mountains."[22]

Barrett Willoughby brought background and skill to her writing, working diligently at her craft. She recorded an Alaskan time when few others did, fostering the romantic image of the northland. Willoughby quoted a Russian author when she said:

I take pieces of life, gray and dull, and create from them the sweetest legend, for I am a poet.[23]

Epilogue

Barrett Willoughby was the product of her family. Her father, the adventurer, gave her the excitement of new discovery, perhaps the enthusiasm for life. She adored him, deferred to him, and accepted him as ultimate authority. He was the model—for better or worse—for all her serious men friends.

Her mother set a quieter, more practical example for her daughter. She might have been a driving force in a more unobtrusive manner. In the end, both Florences gave way to their husbands, granting them the last word.

Florence Barrett Willoughby had many nicknames. There was Flo or Flossie very early, Do-da for first husband Oliver, and Beau, Billie, Barrie, and Billywillo for later life.

Being a romantic was a major key to Willoughby's personality. After all, by its very nature, romance generates an optimistic attitude; it promotes an idealistic view; it appreciates love over sex; it tolerates weaknesses in others; it permits a certain amount of freedom at some expense to responsibility.

The heroines in Barrett Willoughby's romantic novels could have been Florence as she saw herself or as she wished her life to be. Her heroines were sensitive, fun loving, and young. Their principles were in place at all times, yet each had an adaptable personality. The heroines were also elegant in a sophisticated way, but wore this sophistication casually, and took it for granted. They were slim and, though never beautiful, their looks attracted men. When circumstances got rough, they were strong and loyal. It could well be that Florence cast herself as a heroine, for many of these attributes were her own.

Everyone who knew her described Willoughby as intelligent. In spite of obstacles, she first worked and studied to give herself an education as best she could. Then, with few occupational skills, she shaped a new career when into her thirties. It was a time in history when society gave limited freedom and encouragement to women in what could be termed "a man's world."

To compete in such a world, and then make a brilliant success of it, certainly showed her to be intelligent. Willoughby worked at being successful—taking writing courses, reading, researching, promoting. In all ways she paid her dues. She took opportunities and made the most of them. Determination and persistence had to be a big part of her life.

People who knew her well called her cheerful and fun loving. She could be sarcastic, as Ollie accused her, but she was always sorry later and apologized. Mainly, Willoughby kept a happy, optimistic attitude, which seemed to support her during more private moments of sadness. She had a good sense of humor and was enthusiastic.

This optimism showed through in most things she did. Not reticent, she loved trying new experiences. When she flew with pilots Ben Eielson or A. A. Bennett she raved about the scenery, the feeling of elation at flying above everything. Being lost in a fog bank was risky—she knew that—but she made an adventure of it. She was a keen observer and noticed everything. Her attention to scenery and description was well evidenced in her books.

This Willoughby optimism wanted to see only the positive elements in Alaska and in life. Her writings tended to shut out negatives, so that in the end, a true, objective picture was not expressed. While Jack London dwelt on sufferings of the wilderness trail, cold, and brutality, Willoughby flipped the coin completely over. Her readers saw sunshine, excitement, the lushness of Alaska, not the cold, the routine, the harshness that were, as well, part of the total picture. Even the villains in her books had an appealing, dashing quality.

If there was a negative about Willoughby, it might have been her need to be attractive to men. A few people hinted at a flirtatious, even forward manner with males. Plainly, Florence did like men, and they were drawn to her. At gatherings, Elsa Pedersen said Barrie was often the center of attention. Men could easily be attracted to her enthusiastic, optimistic and adventurous spirit.

Whether Florence Willoughby's moral code allowed more sexual freedom than mere attraction cannot be determined. Publicly, and certainly through her heroines, Willoughby expressed the accepted moral viewpoint shared by many of her generation. A quote from *Sondra O'Moore* might best express this attitude:

> Though she sought to present to the world the casual, flippant attitude toward romance that characterized her generation, she was well aware that her heart wore the hoop skirts of her grandmother's day. She actually hoped that love would come to her in a tall ship sailing in across the bay to anchor beneath the windows of Echo House.[15]

Primarily, Willoughby was drawn to adventurous men who were fun but tended to concentrate on themselves and disregard their duties. While those around her were weak in taking responsibility, or were unable to, Willoughby accepted it. She took care of her family and her last husband. Financially this left Barrett Willoughby with little security in her later years. Yet with her optimism and determination, she survived with the basics of her life intact.

In turn Barrett Willoughby proved loyal to these same friends and family. Names of people seen in early documents about her life were seen in later documents, too. She kept her friends, who, as her niece said, "adored her." Willoughby cared for those around her—both emotionally and financially—and did it with grace.

One longtime friend, Herb Hilscher, summed up Willoughby's career in her obituary published in the August 7, 1959, issue of the *Anchorage Daily News*:

> Many have been affected by the geography, the people and the texture of Alaska, and will readily tell you why they came and why they stayed.
>
> But there are few persons sensitive and skillful enough to capture this mood and translate it into literature. Most critics agree that Florence Barrett Willoughby was one of these rare people.

Barrett Willoughby is a lady who should not be forgotten.

This photograph reflects the California sophistication Willoughby had attained over the years. She looks the polished, successful author. *Courtesy of Merion Cass Frolich*

Publications by Barrett Willoughby

Florence Barrett Willoughby (1886–1959) wrote under the pen name of Barrett Willoughby when she published her first book in 1922. The pen name consisted of her maiden name, Barrett, and her first husband's last name, Willoughby. Every piece she published had an Alaska backdrop.

In addition to the book and article entries below, Willoughby mentioned publishing in *The Strand* (England), and *Cosmopolitan* magazine, though copies cannot be found. There may be more articles not listed anywhere. Some of the magazine articles were excerpts from her books or were serialized before publication in book form.

Willoughby's books have long been out of print, many with last printings before 1950.

"Interesting Westerners: George Watkins Evans." *Sunset Magazine* (February 1916): 39. [Authority on coal]

"Interesting Westerners: Alice Anderson." *Sunset Magazine* (March 1916): 34–. [Nurse, teacher]

"Katalla Revived." *The All-Alaska Review* (June 1916): 15.

"Interesting Westerners: George Barrett." *Sunset Magazine* (June 1916): 38. [Discoverer of Alaska coal fields]

"Elias Light Is Ready for Business." *The All-Alaska Review* (September/October 1916): 16.

"How Famous Ship Went Down." *The All-Alaska Review* (July 1916): 15.

"Interesting Westerners: Mrs. C. W. Hammond." *Sunset Magazine* (February 1917): 41. [Teacher]

"Oil Development Work in Alaska Slow." *Oil Trade Journal* (May 1917): 101–. [Oil developments in the Katalla region]

"Interesting Westerners: Allan 'Scotty' Allan." *Sunset Magazine* (February 1921): 42–. [Dog sled trail racer]

Where the Sun Swings North. New York and London: Putnam's; New York: A. L. Burt Co., 1922. [355 pages]

Willoughby's first book was dedicated to her mother, "Who can make a tent in the wilderness seem like home."

This novel primarily tells of a prospector and his family becoming marooned on a deserted island off Alaska's coast, and their survival there. The story echoes Willoughby's own experience when she was a young girl and her family was marooned on Middleton Island.

From the beginning, Willoughby's pen name caused some gender confusion, especially until she became known. This was the first of the pieces she published under the name of Barrett Willoughby. She used that name throughout the rest of her career. A review in

Booklist (January 1923) stated: Mr. Willoughby's well-drawn characters have many thrilling adventures amidst surroundings that are graphically described by a native-born Alaskan.

"Interesting Westerners: Father Andrew P. Kashevaroff." *Sunset Magazine* (February 1923): 26–. [Russian priest]

"Interesting Westerners: Walstein G. Smith." *Sunset Magazine* (April 1923): 28–. [First Territorial Treasurer of Alaska]

"The Law of the Trap Line." *The American Magazine* (November 1923).

"A Little Alaskan Schooner Was My Childhood Home." *The American Magazine* (October 1924): 10–. [Willoughby's life on her father's ship, the Middleton Island ordeal, and Katalla.]

Rocking Moon. New York: Putnam's; New York: A. L. Burt Co., 1925. [360 pp.] The book was published serially in *The American Magazine* in 1924 and 1925.
 This novel, set on an island off Kodiak Island, was dedicated to Father Andrew Peter Kashevaroff, who symbolized the Russian influence of the area. It was a romance with two men vying for a village priest's daughter. A fox farm was used as background setting. The plot was fairly "Willoughby formula," but the book gave authentic Alaskan descriptions.
 Rocking Moon was immediately popular, with three printings in the month it came out, April 1925. The novel was made into a movie—the first movie to be made on location in Alaska by a Hollywood studio.

The Fur Trail Omnibus. New York: Grosset and Dunlap, 1925. [Contains *Where the Sun Swings North* and *Rocking Moon.*]

"King of the Arctic Trail." *American* Magazine (August 1925). [Scotty Allan]

"The Devil-Drum." In *The Best Short Stories of 1925*, edited by Edward J. O'Brien. Boston: Small, Maynard & Company, Publishers, 1926. [Previously published in *The Century Magazine*.)

"The Passing Alaskan." *Sunset Magazine* (May 1926): 27–. [Tlingit Indians]

"Challenge of the Sweepstakes Trail." *The American Magazine* (July 1926). [Scotty Allan]

"Father of Pictures Captures the Spell of Alaska." *The American Magazine* (January 1926). [E. W. Merrill]

"The Man Who Put the Midnight Sun to Work." *The American Magazine* (August 1928): 36–. [C. C. Georgeson]

Gentlemen Unafraid. New York: Putnam's, 1928. [285 pp.]
   This nonfiction book was dedicated to Willoughby's third husband, Robert H. Prosser, who died a year after their marriage. It narrated the stories of six Alaskan pioneers: father of the author, Martin Barrett; trailblazer A. M. 'Sandy' Smith; dog sled racer Allan 'Scotty' Allan; coal mining engineer George Evans; steamboat captain Sydney Barrington; and Sitka plant wizard C. C. Georgeson. Some of the biographical sketches were first published in *The American Magazine* in 1927 and 1928.
   Reviews in the 1928 volume of *Book Review Digest* range from "it lacks form" to "admirable objectively" and "she makes all Alaska 'come alive'" to "her book is full of good reading, as well as the history of the Territory from first-hand sources."

"Grand Ball at Sitka: When Alaska Was Russian." *The Century Magazine* (April 1929): 675–.

The Trail Eater: A Romance of the All-Alaska Sweepstakes. New York: Putnam's, 1929. [400 pp.]

A romance, previously published in *The American Magazine.* Though fictional, the author readily stated that the dog racing incidents and the hero were based on the life of "Scotty" Allan, to whom the book was partly dedicated. The plot again used a young girl who had romantic conflicts with two men, which eventually ended happily. The setting was Nome; the sweepstakes were roughly the forerunner of the Iditarod Trail Sled Dog races later in the twentieth century.

Most reviews of the book were high praise. *The New York Times* review approached the book more critically: "The closing hundred and fifty pages of the story, which deal solely with the progress of the race, are intensely vivid and exciting, but might have been even better had the two hundred and fifty pages of Frozen North melodrama preceding them undergone drastic pruning."

Hubbard, Bernard. "Volcanoes Packed in Ice." In *The Saturday Evening Post* (23 August 1930), edited by Florence Barrett Willoughby, 18–. Reprinted in Hoke, Helen. *Alaska, Alaska, Alaska.* New York: Franklin Watts, 1960.

Sitka: Portal to Romance. Boston: Houghton Mifflin, 1930. [233 pp.] Simultaneous publication under the title, *Sitka: To Know Alaska One Must First Know Sitka.* London: Hodder and Stoughton, 1930. [248 pp.]

The book was part travelogue, part romance, and part history of Sitka. It was written after a visit by the author and a woman friend, Mrs. Kay Van Buren.

A review in the 1930 volume of *Book Review Digest* seems to best characterize the book:

"A chatty book, very informative nevertheless, and good reading. It is a description of Sitka in the light of its Russian and Indian past, especially its Russian past. A good piece of journalism, this book is hardly of reference grade, but might well be read by anyone contemplating an inside voyage to South Eastern Alaska."

"Moon Craters of Alaska." *The Saturday Evening Post* (13 December 1930): 10. [Interview with glacier priest, Bernard Hubbard]

Spawn of the North. New York: Triangle Books [347 pp.]; Boston: Houghton Mifflin [349 pp.]; New York: Grosset & Dunlap [349 pp.], 1932.

This is a romantic/adventure novel of the salmon industry and fish pirates set in and near Ketchikan, Alaska. The heroine was a young daring girl caught between two loves. The plot was a bit more complex than her other novels, but with a similar formula. The novel ran serially in *Cosmopolitan* magazine before being printed in book form. Willoughby's father, Martin Barrett, received the dedication.

In an August 1938 narrative, Willoughby tells of writing the book, and of her fascination with the salmon run:

"It is a wild, spectacular thing—the Salmon run.... At that time, the air, the water, the forests—everything is vibrant with the stir of procreation....[E]ven the men and women go a little mad with love."

Paramount made this book into a motion picture in 1938. The movie version of this novel starred George Raft as the villainous fish pirate. The character was patterned after a friend of Willoughby's who was "a daring, laughing man, much too delightful...."

Alaskans All. Boston: Houghton Mifflin, 1933. Reprint, Freeport, New York: Books for Libraries Press, 1971. [234 pp.]

This nonfiction book included biographical sketches of five Alaskans: pilot Ben Eielson; pioneer innkeeper Harriet Pullen; ice-pilot Louis Lane; priest and geologist Father Bernard Hubbard; and editor "Stroller" White.

Most of these sketches had been previously published in magazines. *Alaskans All* was dedicated to Barrett Willoughby's stepfather—Charles L. Willoughby—who was not only her stepfather but who was an older half-brother to her first husband, Oliver.

A reviewer in *The Boston Transcript* (June 1933) stated: "It is a book to keep one wide awake o' nights for hours after reading it."

"Lighthouse Keeper at the End of West." *The Saturday Evening Post* (26 January 1935): 8–. [Ted Pedersen]

"Log of the New Pioneers." *The Saturday Evening Post* (29 June 1935): 23–. [Argonauts of 1935 in the Matanuska Valley]

River House. Boston: Little, Brown, 1936. Reprint, New York: Triangle Books, November 1942. [389 pp.]

This novel was a romantic adventure set in a hunting lodge near the Canadian/Alaskan border of Southeastern, Alaska. Conflicts of romance again weave themselves through indecision as to whether to marry a wealthy suitor, or a "reckless and daring" steamboat captain. The heroine marries, and finally falls under the spell of River House where she remains rather than return to the comforts of San Francisco.

1936 *Book Review Digest* reviews were very positive, extolling Willoughby's characters and setting. One reviewer, however, said, "Miss Willoughby writes with engaging enthusiasm, though often she is guilty of overwriting...."

This novel, too, was immediately popular, being reprinted three times the April 1936 month it appeared.

River House was published in *The American Magazine* as "The Captive Bride," before coming out in book form.

Johnson, Mrs. Victor. "I'm a Cream-puff Pioneer." In *The American Magazine*, edited by Florence Barrett Willoughby (June 1937): 10–.

"Dwellers in the House of Sleep," *The Alaska Sportsman* (August 1938): 12–. [A shortened, lightly edited version of the same narrative in Willoughby's book, *Alaska Holiday*.]

Sondra O'Moore. Boston: Little, Brown; New York: Grosset and Dunlap, 1939. [320 pp.]

Rival families and loves combine to create this adventure story set in the Sitka area. (Willoughby said she patterned Sondra after her redheaded niece and namesake, Florence Barrett, her brother Lawrence's daughter.) It includes a Japanese spy, valuable stolen charts, smuggling, and exciting action.

The book was dedicated to Willoughby's fourth husband, Captain Larry O'Connor, whom Willoughby divorced three years after the book was published. *Sondra O'Moore* appeared under the title "Lover Come Back" in *The American Magazine* before the book.

The New York Times said, "It [the book] works hard at being mighty exciting, and succeeds pretty well...."

Alaska Holiday. Boston: Little, Brown, 1940. [296 pp.]

Nearly half of the book related Willoughby's adventures in Kodiak during a trip there with a friend. The other half told a series of Alaskan stories considering ghosts, totems, seals, lighthouses, volcanoes, caribou, and sourdoughs. Some of the narratives were printed in magazines before or after book publication. *Alaska Holiday* was the second book dedicated to her mother.

The value in this nonfiction volume was in its story and descriptions, not in its dates or strict historical accuracy.

The *New Yorker* (May 1940) reviewed the book thus: "Miss Willoughby writes with zip and charm and while this is not a travel book in the staid sense of the word, it does take the reader traveling to strange and interesting and little-known places."

"One Alaska Night." *Reader's Digest* (February 1943): 51–. [This was a condensed version of a ghost story appearing in *Alaska Holiday*.]

The Golden Totem: A Novel of Modern Alaska. Boston: Little, Brown, 1945. [315 pp.]

The mining town of Juneau, Alaska, was the setting of the *Golden Totem*, a suspense mystery. The heroine was caught between loves of conflicting personalities, while the plot was filled with deception and misunderstanding, i.e., the Golden Totem mine was being taken over through questionable means. For the first time in her novels, Willoughby does not have an Alaskan heroine, but brings her up from the States as a cheechako [a newcomer to the north].

Whereas Willoughby had been producing material every three years or less since her writing career began, there were five years between *Alaska Holiday* and this, her last full adult book. Perhaps the dedication in *The Golden Totem*—"To a cheerful, disenchanted lady—myself"—reflected her love disappointments and her age, which was approaching sixty. The book had a good reception; it was reprinted four times within three months of the original publication.

Among other comments, *The New York Times* said, "There is a great deal of plot, some spirited action and a smattering of authentic atmosphere...."

Hewitt, John. "The Snow Woman and Mary Hewitt." With Barrett Willoughby. *The Alaska Sportman* (December 1953): 22–. [Extreme cold weather can cause strange thoughts and actions on the trail.]

"Papa Came C.O.D." *Good Housekeeping* (July 1956): 58–. [Martin Barrett, the pull of his adventurous nature, and its affect on family life.]

"The Silent City." *The Alaska Sportsman* (June 1959): 33–. [Dick Willoughby—no relation—sold a mirage photograph to tourists.]

Chandler, Edna W. *Pioneer of Alaskan Skies: The Story of Ben Eielson.* With Barrett Willoughby. New York: Ginn & Company, 1959. [179 pp.]

A juvenile book about Carl Ben Eielson, well known Alaskan bush pilot. Willoughby actually knew and flew with Eielson in earlier years. This book was published several months after Barrett Willoughby's death.

Notes

Chapter 1 - A True Alaskan

1. "*Spawn of the North* by Barrett Willoughby is Highly Interesting," *Alaska Weekly*, 29 April 1932.

2. "*Where the Sun Swings North* Latest Novel," *Cordova Daily Times*, 24 June 1922.

3. *Cosmopolitan* Magazine publicity, 11 June 1931, University of Alaska, Archives, Willoughby Paper; Ibid.; *Town and Country Review* (undated, 1938?); "Alaska's Own Author Is Acquiring Fame," *Stroller's Weekly*, 27 July 1929.

Chapter 2 - A Father's Legacy

1. Barrett Willoughby, *Gentlemen Unafraid* (New York: G. P. Putnam's Sons, 1928), 5.

2. Barrett Willoughby, *The Golden Totem* (Boston: Little, Brown and Co., 1945).

3. Barrett Willoughby, *Rocking Moon* (New York: A. L. Burt Co., 1925).

4. Barrett Willoughby, *Sondra O'Moore* (Boston: Little, Brown and Co., 1939).

5. Thirteenth Census of the United States, Population—Alaska, Second District, Katalla (1910).

6. Barrett Willoughby, *Gentlemen Unafraid* (New York: G. P. Putnam's Sons, 1928), 5–6.

7. Thirteenth Census, Alaska (1910).

8. "Martin Barrett's Experiences," *Cordova Daily Alaska*, 30 November 1912.

9. Ibid.

10. Twelveth Census of the United States, Population—Washington, King County, Seattle (1900).

11. Thirteenth Census, Alaska (1910).

12. Flo Willoughby letter to Nordlinger, 4 July 1942, Willoughby Papers, University of Alaska Fairbanks, Rasmuson Library, Archives. In this letter, Willoughby wrote:

> About my age, it wasn't that I didn't want any one to know, Bouquet, but that I don't know, and mamma doesn't know the year I was born in. I've had a hell of a time all these years when it has been necessary to put age down on anything—because I have a leeway of about five years, and I've used the age most convenient. There is no birth certificate where I was born apparently. And I've had to take any year convenient—sometimes a year that belonged to someone else. . . . I'm your Auntie Beau—that's all that counts—and no matter what year or in what place I was born. Or who brought me into the world.

13. *Town and Country Review*, undated, Willoughby Papers, University of Alaska Fairbanks, Rasmuson Library, Archives.

14. Helen Smith Scudder letter to the author, 23 July 1984.

15. Thirteenth Census, Alaska (1910).

16. "Martin Barrett's Experiences," *Cordova Daily Alaska*, 30 November 1912.

17. Barrett Willoughby, *Sitka: Portal to Romance* (Boston: Houghton Mifflin Company, 1930), 17.

18. Willoughby, *Gentlemen Unafraid*, 4–39.

19. Ibid., 8–9.

20. Donald J. Orth, *Dictionary of Alaska Place Names* (Washington, D.C.: U.S. Government Printing Office, 1967), 500.

21. Willoughby, *Gentlemen Unafraid*, 27.

22. "Stories of Old Pioneers," *Katalla Herald*, 31 August 1907.

23. Willoughby, *Gentlemen Unafraid*, 28.

24. "Application for Grant for Placer Mining," 14 September 1897, Yukon Department of Tourism and Recreation and Culture, Whitehorse, Yukon Territory, Canada.

25. *Polk's Alaska-Yukon Gazetteer* (Seattle: R. L. Polk & Co.'s, Inc., 1901, Dawson).

26. Ibid., 1901, 1902.

27. Craig Family private papers, Dawson, Yukon Territory, Canada, 1901. Yukon Department of Tourism and Recreation and Culture, Whitehorse, Yukon Territory, Canada.

28. *Polk's Alaska-Yukon Gazetteer*, 1902.

29. Twelveth Census of the United States, Washington, 1900.

30. Holy Names Academy, Seattle (Dees to the author, 13 October 1992).

31. Hanson letter to the author, 15 May 1984. Archdiocese, Chancery Archives, Colma, California.

32. Willoughby, *Gentlemen Unafraid*, 38.

Chapter 3 – A Settled Home in Katalla

1. Lone E. Janson, *The Copper Spike* (Anchorage: Alaska Northwest Publishing Co., 1975), 34–39.

2. Orth, *Dictionary of Alaska Place Names*, 500.

3. *Polk's Alaska Gazetteer and Business Directory*, Katalla, 1905–1906.

4. *Catalla Drill*, 26 December 1903, reprinted in the *Cordova Daily Times*, 25 January 1930.

5. "History of the Precinct," *Katalla Herald*, 10 August 1907.

6. *Catalla Drill*, 21 December 1903, reprinted in the *Cordova Daily Times* 20 January 1930.

7. "O. L. Willoughby Locates Much Land But Loses a Valuable Skunk," *Morning Leader* (Port Townsend, Washington), 13 January 1903.

8. *Catalla Drill* (1 February 1903, probably 1904) reprinted in The *Cordova Daily Times*, 1 February 1930.

9. Twelveth Census of the United States, Population of Washington State, Jefferson County, Port Townsend, 1900.

10. "Willoughbys Out on Visit," *Alaska Weekly* (Seattle), 15 June 1923.

11. *Polk's Alaska Gazetteer*, 1907–1908.

12. "Local and Personal," *Katalla Herald*, 4 February 1908.

13. Helen Smith Scudder to the author, 18 August 1984.

14. Janson, *The Copper Spike*, 18.

15. Ibid., 35.

16. KGO radio interview, 14 May 1925, Willoughby Papers, University of Alaska Fairbanks, Rasmuson Library, Archives.

17. "R. S. Stroud Kills Charles F. Damer," *Katalla Herald*, 30 January 1909. At age 18, Robert Stroud sailed north from Washington State to Katalla to work on the railroad for several years. He then moved south to Juneau, Alaska, where he killed a man, beginning his long and well known prison career.

18. "Man Who Spent 43 Years in Solitary Asks Freedom," *Topeka Journal* (Kansas), 25 November 1959.

19. (Advertisement) *Katalla Herald*, 10 August 1907.

20. "Local and Personal, *Katalla Herald*, 4 April 1908.

21. "Personal," *Katalla Herald*, 21 September 1907.

22. "Pioneers Organize," *Katalla Herald*, 24 August 1907.

23. "Analyses of Coal," *Katalla Herald*, 31 October 1908.

24. "Local and Personal," *Katalla Herald*, 4 February 1908.

25. *Katalla Herald*, 23 December 1907.

26. *Katalla Herald*, 4 February 1908.

27. Scudder to the author, 23 July 1984.

28. Florence Willoughby letter to Oliver Willoughby, 24 February 1916, Willoughby Papers, Jefferson County Historical Society, Port Townsend, Washington.

Chapter 4 - Winds of Change

1. Emma Davis, "Katalla and Cordova: Alaska Sojourn," *Alaska Sportsman Magazine* (January 1965): 30–33.

2. Janson, *The Copper Spike*, 54.

3. *Facts About Alaska—The Alaska Almanac—*1980 Edition (Anchorage: Alaska Northwest Publishing Company, 1979), 39.

4. "Local and Personal," *Katalla Herald*, 24 July 1909.

5. "Katalla Oil Is Displacing Other Fuel," *Cordova Daily Alaska*, 18 November 1914.

6. F. Willoughby letter to O. Willoughby, 11 October 1913, Willoughby Papers, Jefferson County Historical Society, Port Townsend, Washington.

7. "Much Activity in Katalla Oil Field," *The Pioneer* (Valdez), March 1921, 21.

8. F. Willoughby letter to O. Willoughby, 9 October 1913, Willoughby Papers, Jefferson County Historical Society, Port Townsend, Washington.

9. "Martin Barrett's Experiences," *Cordova Daily Alaskan*, 30 November 1912.

10. "Happenings In Neighborhood," *Chitna Leader*, 11 March 1913.

11. "Local Brevities," *Valdez Daily Prospector*, 23 June 1913.

12. F. Willoughby letter to O. Willoughby, 9 October 1913, Willoughby Papers, Jefferson County Historical Society.

13. "Capt. Charles Willoughby Passes Away In California," *Alaska Weekly*, 21 January 1938.

14. F. Willoughby letter to O. Willoughby, 20 January 1914, Willoughby Papers, Jefferson County Historical Society.

15. Ibid., November 1913.

16. Ibid.

17. Ibid., 17 December 1913.

18. Ibid., 11 August 1914.

19. *Polk's Alaska Gazetteer*, Katalla 1917–1918.

20. F. Willoughby letter to O. Willoughby, 11 August 1914, Willoughby Papers, Jefferson County Historical Society.

21. Ibid., 29 June 1914.

22. Ibid., 11 August 1914.

23. Ibid.

24. Ibid., 29 June 1914.

25. Ibid., 4 September 1915.

26. Ibid.

27. "Katalla Revived," *All-Alaska Review* (June 1916): 15; "How Famous Ship Went Down," (July 1916): 15; "Katalla," (September/October 1916): 9–10; "Elias Light Is Ready for Business," (September/October 1916): 16; "Katalla Oil," (December 1916): 17.

28. F. Willoughby letter to O. Willoughby, 4 September 1915.

29. Ibid.

30. "Interesting Westerners: George Watkin Evans," *Sunset Magazine*, February 1916.

31. "Interesting Westerners: Alice Anderson," *Sunset Magazine*, March 1916.

32. "Interesting Westerners: George Barrett," *Sunset Magazine*, June 1916.

33. "Accomplished Katalla Lady Visiting Seward Friends," *Cordova Alaska Times*, 16 September 1916.

34. Divorce decree, 16 April 1917. Superior Court, State of Washington, County of Jefferson, Port Townsend, Washington. It is interesting to note that Florence Willoughby's subsequent marriage to Roger Summy might have been illegal. Part of the Willoughby vs. Willoughby *Decree*

of Divorce stated, "It is further ordered and adjudged that each of the parties to this action is hereby prohibited from marrying a third person within six months from the entry of this decree." Yet Florence married Summy only two and a half months after the decree.

35. F. Willoughby letter to O. Willoughby, 24 February 1917, Willoughby Papers, Jefferson County Historical Society.

36. Ibid.

37. "Willoughby to Put Up a Fight for His Claims," *Seward Weekly Gateway*, 4 June 1913.

38. Thirteenth Census of the United States, Population—Alaska, Second District, Katalla, (1910).

39. Marriage certificate, 4 July 1917. Alaska Department of Vital Statistics, Juneau.

40. Willoughby divorce decree, 16 April 1917.

41. Scudder to the author, 11 September 1984.

42. F. Willoughby letter to O. Willoughby, 17 April 1918, Willoughby Papers, Jefferson County Historical Society.

43. "Anchorage Man Is Killed at Casper," *Anchorage Daily Times*, 28 October 1917; "Details of the Killing of Anchorageite," *Anchorage Daily Times*, 9 May 1918. The *Casper Daily Tribune*, 30 October 1917 and 6 November 1917 reported that "Seattle Bessie" Fisher had followed the Barrett Family to Casper to reclaim her car and jewelry. Bessie, declaring that Lawrence carried a gun, bought one herself for protection. They confronted each other, with Mrs. Barrett and her child present, and Bessie shot Lawrence on October 26, 1917. A resulting jury the following May brought in a verdict of "Not guilty" against Bessie Fisher.

44. "Bessie Fisher Shoots to Kill Man She Loves," *The Casper Record*, 30 October 1917. Wyoming Historical Research & Publications, Cheyenne, 22 December 1992.

45. Ibid., "Mother and Widow of Lawrence Barrett Leave for Port Townsend," 6 November 1917.

46. F. Willoughby letter to O. Willoughby, 17 April 1918, Willoughby Papers, Jefferson County Historical Society.

47. Ibid., 8 June 1918.

48. Ibid.

49. Speech, Pacific Coast Woman's Press Assoc., 1925–1926(?), Willoughby Papers, University of Alaska Fairbanks, Rasmuson Library, Archives.

50. F. Willoughby letter to O. Willoughby, October 1918, Willoughby Papers, Jefferson County Historical Society.

51. Ibid.

52. Ibid., 9 October 1918. According to the June 1925 *Pathfinder*, Roger Summy moved to Odell Lake, Oregon, and worked in the general merchandise business.

53. Ibid., 16 September 1918.

54. Ibid., 22 December 1918.

55. Ibid., 3 February 1919.

56. Ibid., 30 January 1920.

Chapter 5 - A First Romantic Novel

1. *Call Bulletin* interview, 4 December 1936, Willoughby Papers, University of Alaska Fairbanks, Rasmuson Library, Archives.

2. F. Willoughby letter to O. Willoughby, 30 January 1920, Willoughby Papers, Jefferson County Historical Society.

3. Fred Willoughby obituary, 21 May 1946. Jefferson County Historical Society, Port Townsend, Washington. Oliver Willoughby traveled to Oregon for awhile, and possibly other locations in the west. The last documented evidence of him was mentioned in his brother Fred's Port Townsend obituary dated 21 May 1946. At that time, Oliver was living in Lumby, British Columbia, Canada, and was almost seventy-seven years old.

4. F. Willoughby letter to O. Willoughby, 19 August 1920, Willoughby Papers, Jefferson County Historical Society.

5. Ibid., 3 July 1920.

6. Radio Talk, 11 June 1931, Willoughby Papers, University of Alaska Fairbanks, Rasmuson Library, Archives.

7. Ibid., 3 July 1920.

8. Scudder to the author, 23 July 1984.

9. F. Willoughby letter to O. Willoughby, August 1920, Willoughby Papers, Jefferson County Historical Society.

10. Nadia Lavrova, "Alaska Girl Writes Novel of Home Land," *San Francisco Chronicle* Library, 9 April 1925. *Town and Country Review* (Undated), Willoughby Papers, University of Alaska Fairbanks, Rasmuson Library, Archives. Marian A. Knight, ed., *Book Review Digest* (New York: H. W. Wilson Co., 1927), 836.

11. "Alaska Is Mecca for Journalist," *Alaska Dispatch, Golden Spike edition* 4 August 1922.

12. "Writer Here Gives Secret, Being Herself Wins Fame," *Seattle Times,* 5 October 1927, Willoughby Papers, University of Washington Libraries, Special Collections, Seattle.

13. Florence Willoughby letter to Florence Rowland, 7 October 1939, Willoughby Papers, University of Alaska Fairbanks, Rasmuson Library, Archives.

14. Lavrova, *San Francisco Chronicle* Library, 19 April 1925.

15. Ernie Smith radio interview, 1932(?), Willoughby Papers, University of Alaska Fairbanks, Rasmuson Library, Archives.

16. Boat Parade interview, 6 April 1935, Willoughby Papers, University of Alaska Fairbanks, Rasmuson Library, Archives.

17. Lavrova, *San Francisco Chronicle* Library, 26 November 1922.

18. Radio interview, 1936(?), Willoughby Papers, University of Alaska Fairbanks, Rasmuson Library, Archives.

19. Ibid., Radio talk, 11 June 1931.

20. Ibid., Boat Parade interview, 6 April 1935.

21. "Alaska, Land of Romance, Beauty," *San Francisco Chronicle,* 4 May 1934, Willoughby Papers, California State Library Collection, Sacramento.

22. "Noted Writer Visits Sitka after Data," *Sitka Tribune,* 23 June 1922.

23. "Noted Alaska Writer Visits Wrangell," *The Wrangell Sentinel,* 4 August 1927.

24. "Juneau To Be Locale Story By Willoughby," *Daily Alaska Empire,* 27 July 1936.

25. Adams interview, undated—1932(?), Willoughby Papers, University of Alaska Fairbanks, Rasmuson Library, Archives.

26. Ibid., Adams interview, 1924–1925.

27. Carol Beery Davis in personal interview with author, 9 April 1984, Juneau, Alaska.

28. Ibid.

29. Lavrova, *San Francisco Chronicle* Library, 26 November 1922.

30. "Is Real Alaskan Book," *The Sitka Tribune,* 22 December 1922.

31. "Where the Sun Swings North," *The Pathfinder*, February 1923.

32. Orth, 500.

33. "Capt. Charles Willoughby Passes Away . . . ," *Alaska Weekly*, 21 January 1938, Willoughby Papers, Jefferson County Historical Society, Port Townsend, Washington.

Chapter 6 - Building a Reputation

1. *Town and Country Review*, (undated, 1938?), Willoughby Papers, University of Alaska Fairbanks, Rasmuson Library, Archives.

2. Ibid., Radio talk, (undated, 1925–26?).

3. "Young Author Believes in Her Hunches," *Ketchikan Alaska Chronicle*, 16 July 1929.

4. Radio talk for *Cosmopolitan*, 11 June 1931, Willoughby Papers, University of Alaska Fairbanks, Rasmuson Library, Archives.

5. Ibid., Adams interview (undated, 1932?).

6. "Alaska, Land of Romance, Beauty," *San Francisco Chronicle*, 4 May 1934, Willoughby Papers, California State Library Collection, Sacramento.

7. Booksellers banquet, 18 April 1929, Willoughby Papers, University of Alaska Fairbanks, Rasmuson Library, Archives.

8. Ibid., NBC radio talk, 6 June 1932.

9. Ibid., Ernie Smith interview, (undated, 1932?).

10. Willoughby, *Sondra O'Moore*, 121.

11. "Alaska, Land of Romance, Beauty," *San Francisco Chronicle*, 4 May 1934, Willoughby Papers, California State Library Collection, Sacramento.

12. Article, untitled, *Sitka Tribune*, 24 September 1925.

13. Lavrova, *San Francisco Chronicle* Library, 9 April 1925.

14. "Finds Color, Romance In Old Kodiak," *Cordova Daily Times*, 13 September 1922.

15. Ibid.

16. Willoughby, *Rocking Moon*, 259.

17. Lavrova, *San Francisco Chronicle* Library, 9 April 1925.

18. Article, untitled, *The Sitka Tribune*, 24 September 1925.

19. "'Rocking Moon' Is Filmed on Schedule," *Alaska Daily Empire*, 2 October 1925.

20. "Local News," *The Sitka Progress*, 26 March 1926.

21. "More Lights on Rocking Moon," *The Sitka Tribune*, 18 December 1925.

22. "Book Cover Designed By Author," *San Francisco Examiner*, July 22, 1928. California State Library, Sacramento.

23. Willoughby, *Gentlemen Unafraid*, 46–47.

24. "'Gentlemen Unafraid' Has Been Chosen as One of Two Greatest Books Recent Years," *Alaska Weekly*, 20 February 1931.

25. *Who was Who in America*, Vol. III, 1951–1960 (Chicago: Marquis Who's Who, Inc., 1960), 924.

26. "Barrett Willoughby, Alaska Novelist, Dies," *Daily Alaska Empire*, 30 July 1959.

27. Death certificate, Robert Prosser, June 9, 1928. Pennsylvania Division of Vital Records, New Castle.

28. Scudder letter to the author, 23 June 1984.

29. Prosser death certificate, June 9, 1928.

30. Willoughby, *The Trail Eater*, back of title page.

31. Willoughby, *The Trail Eater*, foreward.

32. "'Scotty' Allan, Noted Alaskan In the Pictures," *Alaska Weekly*, 23 November 1928.

33. Review of *The Trail Eater*, in *The New York Times*, 7 July 1929. (*Book Review Digest*, 1929.)

34. B. Willoughby letter to Mr. and Mrs. White, (19 or 20 November, year unknown). Bancroft Library, University of California, Berkeley.

35. Willoughby, *Sitka: Portal to Romance*, 127.

36. W. B. Shaw review of *Sitka: Portal to Romance* in R of Rs, 30 May 1930. (*Book Review Digest*, 1930, page 1128.)

Chapter 7 – A Seasoned Author

1. KGO radio talk, 16 May 1932, Willoughby Papers, University of Alaska Fairbanks, Rasmuson Library, Archives.

2. Ibid.

3. *Cosmopolitan* publicity, 11 June 1931, Willoughby Papers, University of Alaska Fairbanks, Rasmuson Library, Archives.

4. Interview with Ernie Smith (undated, 1932?), Willoughby Papers, University of Alaska Fairbanks, Rasmuson Library, Archives.

5. Librarian Convention speech, 25 February 1933, Willoughby Papers, University of Alaska Fairbanks, Rasmuson Library, Archives.

6. Ibid.

7. *Cosmopolitan* publicity, 11 June 1931, Willoughby Papers, University of Alaska Fairbanks, Rasmuson Library, Archives.

8. Interview with Ernie Smith (undated, 1932?), Willoughby Papers, University of Alaska Fairbanks, Rasmuson Library, Archives.

9. "Barrett Willoughby Out With New Book," *Stroller's Weekly*, 30, June 1929.

10. Review of *Spawn of the North* in *Booklist*, June 1932. (*Book Review Digest*, 1932, page 1031.)

11. "Bad Luck Dogs Footsteps of Motion Picture Men," *Ketchikan Alaska Chronicle*, 1 July 1936.

12. "Complete Cast for Picture Is Still Undecided," *Ketchikan Alaska Chronicle,*16 June 1936.

13. Ibid., 1 July 1936.

14. Richard Bertrand Dimmitt, *A Title Guide to the Talkies* (New York: Scarecrow Press, 1965), 26.

15. "Anan Scenes Filmed for New Picture," *Wrangell Sentinel,* 10 September 1937.

16. *Spawn of the North* photo stills, 1939, Academy of Motion Picture Arts and Sciences, Beverly Hills, California.

17. "Alaska, Land of Romance, Beauty," *San Francisco Chronicle,* 4 May 1934. California State Library Collection, Sacramento.

18. Willoughby, *Spawn of the North,* 5.

19. Willoughby, *Sitka: Portal to Romance,* 4.

20. Barrett Willoughby notes, (undated 1932?), Willoughby Papers, University of Alaska Fairbanks, Rasmuson Library, Archives.

21. Ibid.

22. "Writer Here Gives Secret, Being Herself Wins Fame," *Seattle Times,* 5 October 1927, Special Collections. University of Washington Libraries, Seattle.

23. Mr. Adams interview (undated, 1932?), Willoughby Papers, University of Alaska Fairbanks, Rasmuson Library, Archives.

24. Ibid.

25. Ibid.

26. "Death of Alaska Authoress Ends Talented Career," Anchorage *Daily News,* 7 August 1959.

27. Florence Willoughby letter to Irving Shepard, 4 February 1956, Jack London Papers. The Henry E. Huntington Library and Art Gallery, San Marino, California.

28. "Old Russian History," *Alaska Weekly,* 30 November 1923.

29. "Alaska's Own Author Is Acquiring Fame," *Stroller's Weekly,* 27 July 1929.

30. F. Willoughby to Florence Rowland, 7 October 1939, Willoughby Papers, University of Alaska Fairbanks, Rasmuson Library, Archives.

31. Ibid.

32. Library Convention, 25 February 1933, Willoughby Papers, University of Alaska Fairbanks, Rasmuson Library, Archives.

33. F. Willoughby to F. Rowland, 7 October 1939, Willoughby Papers, University of Alaska Fairbanks, Rasmuson Library, Archives.

Chapter 8 - Height of Her Career

1. Scudder letter to the author, 23 July 1984.

2. Librarian convention, 25 February 1933, Willoughby Papers, University of Alaska Fairbanks, Rasmuson Library, Archives.

3. Ibid.

4. Willoughby, *Alaskans All*, 104.

5. Ibid., 213.

6. C. L. Skinner, review of *Alaskans All, Books*, 30 April 1933, in *Book Review Digest* (1934): 1025.

7. *Call Bulletin* interview, 4 December 1936, Willoughby Papers, University of Alaska Fairbanks, Rasmuson Library, Archives.

8. Willoughby, *River House*, back of title page.

9. *Alaska Weekly*, 19 July 1935 (picture). James Wickersham, *A Bibliography of Alaskan Literature 1724–1924.* (Cordova: Cordova Daily Times for Alaska Agricultural College and School of Mines Fairbanks, 1927), 276.

10. "Thru Northern Glasses," *Alaska Weekly*, 21 March 1930.

11. Paul Elder interview, 18 April 1936, Willoughby Papers, University of Alaska Fairbanks, Rasmuson Library, Archives.

12. Willoughby, *River House*, paper jacket flap.

13. Radio talk, (undated, 1939?), Willoughby Papers, University of Alaska Fairbanks, Rasmuson Library, Archives.

14. *The New York Times*, 29 March 1936, in *Book Review Digest* (1936): 1047.

15. *Boston Transcript*, 9 May 1936.

16. Barrett Willoughby, "Critics Called Her a He-Villain," *San Francisco Chronicle*, 2 December 1923. California State Library Collection, Sacramento.

17. Ibid.

18. Mrs. Paul Charles (Ketchikan) letter to the author, 14 April 1984. Phone conversations, Robert DeArmond to the author, 13 July 1984, 6 September 1992.

19. Phone conversation, Elsa Pedersen to the author, 15 September 1993.

20. Marriage certificate, Larry O'Conner and Florence Prosser, 17 July 1935. State of Nevada, County of Washoe, Reno, Nevada.

21. Radio talk, (undated, 1939?), Willoughby Papers, University of Alaska Fairbanks, Rasmuson Library, Archives.

22. Ibid., radio talk, 3.

23. Willoughby, *The Golden Totem*, 4–5.

24. Phone conversation, Elsa Pedersen to the author, 17 September 1993.

25. Ibid.

26. "Capt. Charles Willoughby Passes Away in California," *Alaska Weekly*, 21 January 1938.

27. Phone conversation, Elsa Pedersen to the author, 17 September 1993.

28. "Books," *San Francisco Chronicle*, 19 November 1939. California State Library Collection, Sacramento.

29. "O'Moore Latest Novel Willoughby," *Alaska Weekly*, 28 September 1939.

30. Willoughby, *Sondra O'Moore*, 319.

31. Ibid., back of title page.

32. Beaverton Book Club talk (undated, 1939?), Willoughby Papers, University of Alaska Fairbanks, Rasmuson Library, Archives.

33. Florence Nordlinger to the author, 26 November 1988.

34. Ibid., 9 January 1989.

35. Ibid.

36. "One Alaska Night," *Reader's Digest*, February 1943.

37. "I'm a Cream-puff Pioneer," *The American Magazine*, June 1937.

38. "Barrett Willoughby's Latest Alaskan Holiday Now on Sale," *Alaska Weekly*, 10 May 1940.

39. Willoughby, *Alaska Holiday*, 194–95.

40. Review of *Alaska Holiday*, *New Yorker* magazine, 11 May 1940, in *Book Review Digest* (1940): 995.

41. Phone conversation, Carol Sturgulewski to the author, 17 September 1993.

42. Phone conversation, Elsa Pedersen to the author, 15 September 1993.

43. Ibid.

44. Elsa Pederson, *Dangerous Flight* (New York: Abingdon Press, 1960).

Chapter 9 - A "Disenchanted Lady"

1. Letter, Elsa Pedersen to the author, 13 September 1993.

2. *Who was Who In America* (Chicago: Marquis Who's Who, Inc., 1960), 924.

3. Barrett Willoughby letter to Beau Nordlinger, 4 July 1942, Willoughby Papers, University of Alaska Archives, Fairbanks.

4. Phone conversation, Elsa Pedersen to the author, 17 September 1993.

5. Barrett Willoughby letter to Beau Nordlinger, 4 July 1942, Willoughby Papers, University of Alaska Archives, Fairbanks.

6. Ibid.

7. Ibid.

8. Ibid.

9. Ibid.

10. Mr. Jackson radio talk, 20 May 1925–26, Willoughby Papers, University of Alaska Fairbanks, Rasmuson Library, Archives.

11. Willoughby, *The Golden Totem*, flap on book jacket.

12. Ibid, 5.

13. Review of *The Golden Totem*, *Weekly Book Review*, 18 March 1945, in *Book Review Digest* (1945): 775.

14. Review of the *Golden Totem*, *The New York Times*, 11 March 1945.

15. B. Willoughby letter to Mabel Gillis, 8 April 1945. California State Library, Archives, Sacramento.

16. B. Willoughby letter to Irving Shepard, 8 October 1956, Jack London Papers. The Huntington Library and Art Gallery, San Marino, California.

17. "The Snow Woman and Mary Hewitt," *The Alaska Sportsman*, December 1953.

18. Leslie Halliwell, *Halliwell's Film Guide* (New York; Scribner's Sons, 1986).

19. Pedersen letter to the author, 13 September 1993.

20. Ibid.

21. B. Willoughby letter to Irving Shepard, 4 February 1956, Jack London Papers. The Huntington Library, San Marino.

22. Ibid., 20 November 1955.

23. Ibid., 4 February 1956.

24. Ibid., 23 May 1956.

25. Ibid., 20 November 1955.

26. Ibid., 8 October 1956.

27. Ibid.

28. Ibid.

29. Ibid., 16 January 1957.

30. Ibid.

31. Ibid., 1 May 1956.

32. Death certificate, 29 July 1959. Bureau of Vital Statistics, Sacramento.

33. Nordlinger letter to the author, 9 January 1989.

34. "From Ketchikan to Barrow," *The Alaska Sportsman,* November 1959.

35. Bob Henning phone conversation with the author, 11 October 1993.

Chapter 10 - Inside Willoughby's Books

1. "Her Latest and Her Best," *Alaska Weekly,* 16 November 1928.

2. Willoughby, *Alaskans All,* 16, 18–19.

3. "Old Russian History," *Alaska Weekly,* 30 November 1923.

4. Willoughby, *River House,* 13.

5. Ibid.

6. Ibid., 14.

7. Willoughby, *Gentlemen Unafraid,* 10–11.

8. Willoughby, *The Golden Totem,* 135.

9. Willoughby, *Spawn of the North,* 107.

10. Willoughby, *River House,* 319.

11. Willoughby, *Sondra O'Moore,* 11.

12. Willoughby, *The Trail Eater,* 252.

13. Willoughby, *Rocking Moon,* 206.

14. Willoughby, *Sondra O'Moore,* 59.

15. Willoughby, *Rocking Moon,* 300.

16. Willoughby, *The Golden Totem,* 150.

17. Willoughby, *Spawn of the North,* 133–134.

18. Willoughby, *River House,* 339.

19. Willoughby, *Rocking Moon,* 115.

20. Willoughby, *The Golden Totem,* 271.

21. Willoughby, *The Trail Eater*, 391.

22. Willoughby, *The Golden Totem*, 106–107.

23. *Alaska Weekly*, 30 November 1923.

Bibliography

Manuscript Collections

Alaska State Historical Library, Juneau, Alaska.

Barrett, Lawrence. Papers. Historical Research & Publications, Wyoming Division of Parks and Cultural Resources, Cheyenne, Wyoming.

California Historical Society, San Francisco.

Cordova Historical Society, Cordova, Alaska.

London, Jack. Papers. Henry E. Huntington Library and Art Gallery, San Marino, California.

Regional History Center, University of Southern California, Los Angeles, California.

Spawn of the North. Photo stills. Academy of Motion Picture Arts and Sciences, Beverly Hills, California.

Willoughby, Barrett. Clippings. *San Francisco Chronicle* Library.

Willoughby, Barrett. Entries, December 29, 1992. Archives and Humanities Department, San Francisco Main Library.

Willoughby, Barrett. Papers. Bancroft Library, University of California, Berkeley.

Willoughby, Barrett. Papers. California State Library, Sacramento, California.

Willoughby, Barrett. Papers. Henry E. Huntington Library and Art Gallery, San Marino, California.

Willoughby, Barrett. Papers. Elmer E. Rasmuson Library, Archives, University of Alaska Fairbanks.

Willoughby, Barrett. Papers. Special Collections, University of Washington Libraries, Seattle.

Willoughby, O. L. Papers. Jefferson County Historical Society, Port Townsend, Washington.

Willoughby, Sarah and Charles. Papers. Jefferson County Historical Society, Port Townsend, Washington.

Books

Alaska Atlas & Gazetteer. Freeport, Maine: DeLorme, 1992.

Anchorage Alaska Telephone Directory, 1924.

Book Review Digest. New York: H. W. Wilson Company, 1922, 1925, 1929, 1930, 1933, 1934, 1936, 1937, 1939, 1940, 1945.

Burke, W. J. and Will D. Howe. *American Authors and Books 1640 to the Present Day.* New York: Crown Publishers, Inc., 1972.

Chandler, Edna W. and Barrett Willoughby. *Pioneer of Alaskan Skies: The Story of Ben Eielson.* New York: Ginn and Company, 1959.

Chang, Tohsook P. and Alden M. Rollins, ed. *Anchorage Times Obituary Index, 1915–1965.* Anchorage: University of Alaska, 1979.

Chase, Will H. *Pioneers of Alaska.* Kansas City: Burton Publishing Company, 1951.

Dimmitt, Richard Bertrand. *A Title Guide to the Talkies.* New York: Scarecrow Press, 1965.

Facts About Alaska—The Alaska Almanac, 1980 Edition. Anchorage: Alaska Northwest Publishing Company, 1979.

Graham, Roberta. *A Sense of History—A Reference Guide to Alaska's Women, 1896–1985.* Anchorage: Alaska Women's Commission, 30 June 1985.

Halliwell, Lesie. *Halliwell's Film Guide.* New York: Charles Scribner's Sons, 1986.

Hay, Stephen W. and Betty J. Hay, ed. *Melvin Ricks' Alaska Bibliography.* Portland, Oregon: Binford & Mort for the Alaska Historical Commission, 1977.

Haycox, Stephen W. *A Warm Past: Travels in Alaska History.* Anchorage: Press North, Inc., 1988.

Hellenthal, J. A. *The Alaskan Melodrama.* New York: Liveright Publishing Corporation, 1936.

Hoke, Helen. *Alaska Alaska Alaska.* New York: Franklin Watts, Inc., 1960.

Janson, Lone E. *The Copper Spike.* Anchorage: Alaska Northwest Publishing Company, 1975.

Leahy, Marilyn. *Women of Juneau—1887–1891.* Juneau, Alaska: Alaska Historical Commission, Juneau, Alaska, 198–.

O'Connor, Richard. *Jack London, A Biography.* Boston: Little, Brown & Company, 1964.

O'Cotter, Pat. *Rhymes of a Roughneck.* Seward, Alaska: By the Author, 1918.

Orth, Donald J. *Dictonary of Alaska Place Names.* Washington, D.C.: U.S. Government Printing Office, 1967.

Polk's Alaska-Yukon Gazetteer. Seattle: R. L. Polk & Co.'s, Inc., 1901, 1902, 1903, 1905–06, 1907–08, 1917–18, 1923–24.

Port Townsend and Hadlock Directory—1897. Seattle: Metropolitan Printing & Binding Company.

Ricks, Melvin B. *A Basic Bibliography of Alaskan Literature, Annotated.* Juneau, Alaska: (Type scripted by hand), 1960.

Stone, Irving. *Sailor on Horseback.* Boston: Houghton Mifflin Company, 1938.

Territorial Telephone Books. Juneau and Douglas, Alaska, September 1936.

Tourville, Elsie A. *Alaska, A Bibliography*, 1570–1970. Boston: G. K. Hall & Co., 1974.

Who Was Who Among English and European Authors, 1931–1949. Detroit: Gale Research Company, 1978.

Who Was Who in America, Vol. III, 1951–1960. Chicago: Marquis Who's Who, Inc., 1960.

Wickersham, James. *A Bibliography of Alaskan Literature 1724–1924.* Cordova: *Cordova Daily Times* for Alaska Agricultural College and School of Mines, Fairbanks, 1927.

Articles

"A Real Alaskan Novelist." *The Pathfinder* (May 1922): 21.

Davis, Emma A. "Katalla and Cordova: Alaska Sojourn." *The Alaska Sportsman* (January 1965): 30–33.

DeArmond, Robert. "This Month in Northland History." *The Alaska Sportsman* (November 1968): 18.

DeArmond, Robert. "This Month in Northland History." *The Alaska Sportsman* (April 1968): 26.

"From Ketchikan to Barrow." *The Alaska Sportsman* (November 1959): 22.

Hewitt, John Michael and Barrett Willoughby. "The Snow Woman and Mary Hewitt." *The Alaska Sportsman* (December 1953): 22–24.

"Much Activity in Katalla Oil Field." *The Pathfinder* (March 1921): 21.

Paine, Jean. "Interesting Westerners: A Literary Alaskan." *Sunset* (May 1923): 34–35.

"Sourdough Notes." *The Pathfinder* (March 1924): 16.

"Sourdough Notes." *The Pathfinder* (August 1923): 16.

"Where the Sun Swings North." *The Pathfinder* (February 1923): 9.

Newpapers

The Alaska Catholic, July 31, 1937.

Alaska Daily Empire, December 28, 1920.

The Alaska Dispatch (The Golden Spike Edition), August 4, 1922.

Alaska Prospector (Valdez), January 24, 1907.

Alaska Times (Cordova), September 16, 1916.

Alaska Weekly (Seattle), 1922–1930; 1935–1951.

Anchorage (Alaska) Daily Times, August 7, 1959.

Anchorage (Alaska) Daily Times, February 22, 1917; October 28, 1917; May 9, 1918.

The Casper (Wyoming) Record, October 30, 1917; November 6, 1917.

Chitna Leader (Cordova), March 11, 1913; July 10, 1917.

Cordova Daily Alaskan, October–November 1912; November 1914.

Cordova Daily Times, October 31, 1917; June–September 1922; January–March 1930 (reprint of 1903–1904 *Catalla Drill*).

The Daily Alaska Dispatch, May 17, 1918.

Daily Alaska Empire, September–December 1922; May–August 1922; September–December 1925; October 8, 1928; July–August 1936.

Katalla Herald, August 1907–July 24, 1909.

Ketchikan (Alaska) Chronicle, July 16, 1929; May–September 1937; June–July 1936.

Matanuska Valley Pioneer, August 1936.

Morning Leader (Port Townsend, Washington), January 13, 1903.

The New York Times, July 31, 1959.

Nome (Alaska) Nugget, September 1929.

Russian paper (no masthead). Barrett Willoughby's photograph, May 4, 1929. (San Francisco publication?).

San Francisco Chronicle, April 26, 1925; July 30, 1959.

The San Francisco Examiner, October 28, 1923; November 18, 1923; May 9, 1924.

Seattle Times, October 5, 1927; October 21, 1962.

Seward Gateway, September 1936.

Seward Weekly Gateway, October 10, 1910; June 14, 1913.

Sitka Progress, February–March 1926.

Sitka Tribune, June–July 1922; September–December 1925.

Stroller's Weekly, June 30, 1929; July 27, 1929.

Topeka (Kansas) Journal, November 25, 1959.

Valdez (Alaska) Daily Prospector, June 1913.

Valdez (Alaska) Miner, September 1936.

Wrangell (Alaska) Sentinel, June 28, 1923; August–October 1927; June 26, 1936; September 10, 1937.

Vital Records

Alaska Vital Statistics, Juneau. Marriage certificate, Florence Barrett and Charles Willoughby, 21 June 1913.

Alaska Vital Statistics, Juneau. Marriage certificate, Florence Willoughby and Roger Summy, 4 July 1917.

California State Vital Statistics, Sacramento. Death certificate, Florence Barrett Willoughby Prosser, 29 July 1959.

Fourteenth U.S. Census Records, 1920. Alaska, Washington, Oregon, California.

Jefferson County Clerk's Office, Port Townsend, Washington. Divorce decree, O. L. Willoughby and Florence Willoughby, 16 April 1917.

Pennsylvania Division of Vital Records, New Castle. Death certificate, Robert H. Prosser, 9 June 1928.

Thirteenth U.S. Census Records, 1910. Alaska, Washington, California.

Twelveth U.S. Census Records, 1900. Alaska, Washington.

Washoe County Recorder, Reno, Nevada. Marriage certificate, Florence Prosser and Larry O'Connor, 17 July 1935.

Unpublished

"Annotated Bibliography on Alaska." Juneau: Alaska State Historical Library, 15 June 1954. Machine copy.

Rogers, Janet. "Barrett Willoughby: First Lady of Alaskan Literature." Ph.D. dissertation, University of Alaska, Fairbanks, (undated).

Personal Communications

Atwood, Robert. Telephone conversation with author, October 1992.

Charles, Patricia (Mrs. Paul B.). Letter to author, April 1984.

Davis, Carol Beery. Conversations with author, April 1984.

DeArmond, Robert. Typed notes, personal and phone conversations with author, May, July 1984; September 1992.

Gregg, Inez. Conversations with author, June 1984.

Henning, Bob. Telephone conversation with author, October 11, 1993.

Hilscher, Miriam. Telephone conversation with author, October 1992.

Pedersen, Elsa. Telephone conversations and correspondence with the author, September 1993.

Sturgulewski, Carol. Phone conversations with author, September 1993.

Sullivan, Sister M. Ann. Phone and correspondence with author, September and October 1992.

Houghton Mifflin Company, Boston. Correspondence with author, May 1984.

Little, Brown and Company, Boston. Correspondence with author, March 1989.

Lukas, Mark. Correspondence with author, September 1988.

McDonald, Lucile. Correspondence with author, May and September 1984.

Nordlinger, Florence Barrett. Correspondence with author, November 1988 and January 1989.

Scudder, Helen Smith. Letters and telephone conversations with the author, July, August and September 1984.

Taylor, Christine. Telephone conversation with author, September 28, 1992.

Wiks, Margaret Bell. Correspondence with author, April 1984.

Winn, William. Conversations with author, September 1991.

Index

C

G

Y

Alaska

Barrow

Nome

Unimak Island

Kodia

6

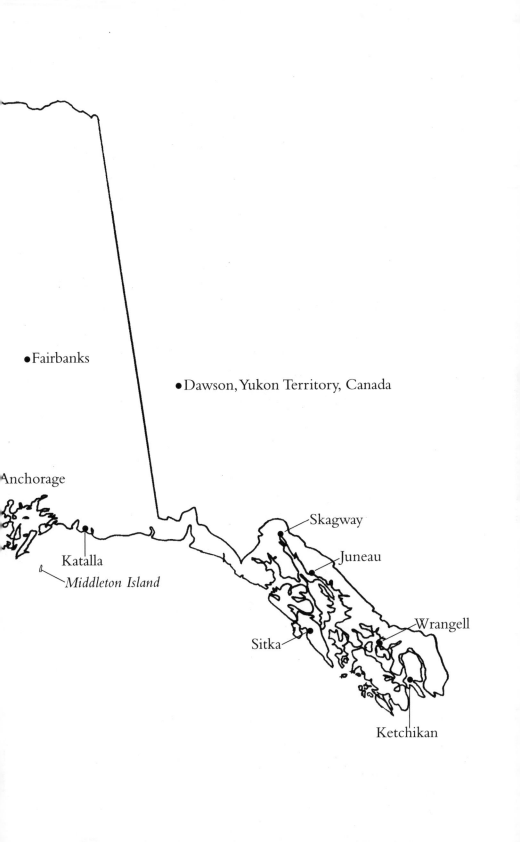

●Fairbanks

●Dawson, Yukon Territory, Canada

Anchorage

Skagway

Juneau

Katalla

Middleton Island

Wrangell

Sitka

Ketchikan

**Nancy Warren Ferrell** is the author of several nonfiction books for young readers and has contributed articles to a variety of adult and juvenile magazines. She has served on numerous writing panels, conducts workshops, and is a member of national and local professional writers' organizations. Ms. Ferrell received her B.A. degree in psychology from Lawrence College, Appleton, Wisconsin.

JEFFERSON COUNTY LIBRARY
620 Cedar Avenue
Port Hadlock, WA 98339
(360) 385-6544   www.jclibrary.info

JEFFERSON COUNTY LIBRARY
620 Cedar Avenue
Port Hadlock, WA 98339
(360) 385-6544 www.jclibrary.info